ISBN 978-1-68517-793-5 (paperback)
ISBN 978-1-68517-794-2 (digital)

Christian Faith Publishing
832 Park Avenue
Meadville, PA 16335
www.christianfaithpublishing.com

Printed in the United States of America

Introduction

"I just had an epiphany!" I exclaim to my little copilots on our way home from Wednesday night Bible study, where we were discussing the book of Acts. "You know how when I've asked God for guidance for my career as a nurse, three times now I've gotten a resounding *write*, and I get totally overwhelmed because I haven't written in my book for years and I have no idea where to start?" I tell my teenage daughter, my sounding board for all my ideas.

"Yes, Mom. I know," she replies. "Well, I realized God wants me to write about *God*!"

Then the word of God spread, and the number of disciples multiplied greatly in Jerusalem, and a great many of the priests were obedient to the faith. (Acts 6:7 NKJV)

For over ten years now, I have been recording many of the significant events in my life with the hope that my experiences, my mistakes, and the lessons I've learned may help someone somehow, no matter how slight. What had me stuck was that it all seemed so disjointed; how could I make it all fit together into tale anyone might be interested in reading? Then it came to me—God is the glue. My journey up to this point, during my forty years on this earth, had all been interwoven by God, regardless if I was aware of it at the time. It was time that I listen to God calling. It was time again to *write*.

God calls us to spread his Word, to share with the world His glory. However, I am not a talker. I am not a preacher. I thought

living my life in the glorious light of God, with the joy and peace emanating from my being, it would be enough for others to see. Now, I realize people can read it in my written words, as well as in the smile on my face.

Joyful Chaos
and
Little Miracles

An Autobiography

RACHEL REAL

Chapter 1

Ask, and it will be given you; seek and you will
find; knock, and it will be opened to you. For
everyone who asks receives, and he who seeks
finds, and to him who knocks it will be opened.
—Matthew 7:7 (NKJV)

In my early adult life, I considered myself spiritual, believing in a higher power, but not believing in Jesus or God as represented in the Bible. I needed tangible evidence of Jesus's existence. I saw the Bible as an elaborate collection of fantastical stories and the miracles that Jesus accomplished as embellished acts intended to brainwash the public. I must admit that at this time my knowledge of the Bible was extremely limited.

My stepdad Larry, who was always dad to me, was a hardworking electrician that did his best to care for me and my mom. He came into our lives when I was seven years old, and we spent most of my childhood moving from apartments, complex to complex, in San Diego. One such complex happened to be across the street from a Baptist church. I struck up an easy friendship with the pastor's daughter, and I began attending church. I was baptized at this church and came to realize my parents were not the religious type. I learned much later that my dad was actually Lutheran and would pray quietly without me ever knowing. Although I attended the church regularly for at least a year, I believe I was more interested in having friends and did not retain much from the lessons. I see now how helpful it is to approach religion as a family unit.

At the age of ten, my attempts at fellowship were overshadowed by a more pressing matter, at least in mine and my family's minds. If

I only knew God as I do now, the discovery of my disease may have been less distressing.

I always felt so tired and constantly hungry but seemed to be losing weight. My mom Andie made an appointment for me to be seen by the pediatrician a month out, but when my fourth-grade teacher contacted my mother concerned that I was needing frequent bathroom breaks, my mom moved up the appointment to a sooner time. My parents were concerned I may have leukemia. I just wanted to take a nap. The test results came back; my blood sugar was well over six hundred, and the doctor reported he believed I would have been in a coma had we waited another week.

A normal blood sugar reading for someone without diabetes is between 80 to 130 mg/dL. I was diagnosed with type 1 diabetes, a chronic condition where your pancreas produces little to no insulin, requiring injections of insulin and frequent testing of blood sugars with finger-sticks to assure good control. My life became centered around what and when I ate, the quantity, location and time of my injections, and battling the denial that I had a disease that would require my constant attention at an age when all I wanted to do was to play with friends.

I didn't mind the insulin injections. I was even excited to learn how to administer my own shots. Looking back, I'm thankful to have been diagnosed so young. I had the luxury of a major lifestyle change before years of habits had time to take hold. Then, as I still do now, I had trouble avoiding the spoons of sugar from the sugar jar. It's no surprise the blood test to measure the average of my blood sugars over the last six months, hemoglobin A1c, frequented the double digits. I lied, and I lied all the time. I was afraid to take my blood sugar knowing it would be high, so I fabricated an elaborate record of normal glucose readings with the occasional lows or highs. I would rotate pens and pencils, recording entire weeks at a time just so that no one would know how little I cared to take care of myself. My mom and dad were always there, caring, concerned. Eventually I came clean after much prodding and pleading from my parents and got a little help. I was in denial.

In adolescence, at least once a week, I suffered from nocturnal hypoglycemic episodes or seizures, most resulting in falls out of bed, frequent trips to the ER for post-seizure migraines—which I discovered as an adult were actually due to the glucagon—and frequent bedding changes due to loss of bladder control. To this day, my diabetes is a constant struggle. I have periods of control, often when my diet consists of very little carbohydrates, and then for no reason my blood sugars trend low. The next week, they are back in the two hundreds and three hundreds.

To help illustrate what a diabetic seizure looks like from the perspective of a loved one, my husband wrote this.

> The first alert that a seizure is coming is the look of confusion, panic, and exclamation coming from my wife. Sometimes she tells me with her voice that her blood sugar is low, but as the seizure hits her, the voice turns into a gargling gasp that sounds as if she is struggling to suck air through a water filled hose. Her skin turns pale. Her eyes and body start turning to the left all together, as if she wants to spin in a circle. Because this has happened a few times while she is standing and looking for her glucose, I must grab her so that she does not fall. Her body feels stiff, like rigor mortis has set in and then the shaking starts. As I lower her to the floor, her body straining to suck in air and making the sound of a horror movie ghoul, I see her eyes and the dread hits me like a rock. Her eyes look as if she has seen her own death, shear fear and panic, and it makes me believe her eyes, that she has died. With this belief in my head, I must react accordingly. Call 911, give her the glucagon shot, support her head, keep her airway open (look up the head-tilt, chin-lift method), then just talk to her. People going through trauma benefit from

a calming voice next to them. It has an unconscious effect of reassurance, and it gives you
something to do while waiting for the paramedics. Usually within several minutes the seizure
stops and she looks as if she is just taking a nap.
I keep talking because in a minute she will wake
up and be confused. Her eyes open, the fear and
panic are replaced by the look of waking up and
not understanding where she is. When I tell her
she has had a seizure I can see that she feels shame
and embarrassment. The last thing I could feel
toward her at this time is shame, I'm just happy
she is alive and talking to me. It doesn't seem possible, but a 10-minute episode like this can make
you feel like you hiked the alps and haven't slept
in 3 days. The adrenaline dump is exhausting.

As a teenager, I attended a different church in San Diego on a
few separate occasions with my dear friend Raine. The experiences
gave me the feeling of terrible certainty that the church's main concern was all about collecting money. During this very impressionable
time in my life, the sermons seemed to be all about tithing. At one
point, the women in the church surrounded me, laying their hands
on my forehead and shoulders, and boisterously requested God to
remove the migraines that I had experienced most of my life. The
migraines continued, and I was left with a very sour feeling in my
heart toward the Christian church.

Throughout high school, I did not pursue my faith. Occasionally
I would engage in discussion about religion, but even then I did not
enjoy debate, so I would more likely avoid the subject altogether.
At the age of seventeen, I met Dustin. He was so different from any
guy I had ever dated. The summer after we graduated from different
schools, he and I began seeing movies with our two mutual friends,
and then eventually we went together alone. I was ready to marry
him after our first date, but alas, he made me wait for another six
years.

Dustin's parents were missionaries, so he grew up in the faith. At the time of our meeting and for the next seven years or so, I considered myself spiritual, but not a Christian. I held a firm belief in a higher power, but at the time, the Bible still felt like a work of fiction. Our wedding officiator included talk of God bringing us together in the speech she showed me prior to the wedding. Given my unsteady belief, I asked her to remove the words, to which she agreed. In the end, she recited those words at our wedding, which at the time irritated me. But now of course I am glad she did. Little did I know at the time how true those words were—God truly blessed me with this wonderful man.

Chapter 2

Becoming a Mom

Every night as a teenager and during my early twenties, I would gaze up at the stars, find the brightest one, and wish with all my heart to be a mother. Once I became pregnant, I wished and prayed for a healthy baby. I love to tell my daughter this whenever she is feeling hopeless.

Dustin and I began seriously talking about starting a family early in our marriage; so under the direction of my trusted endocrinologist Malinda Fox—to this day the only provider who has been able to reach the deep recesses of my mind that need to be tapped to maintain excellent control of my diabetes—we began the planning that included starting an insulin pump. One year prior to becoming pregnant, I started cracking down on the cravings, doing my best to test my glucose frequently throughout the day, and keeping my blood sugars within therapeutic ranges. I had just become a nurse and attained my first position at a skilled nursing facility for people with severe Alzheimer's and dementia, so the stress of my first nursing position and working the night shift taking on far too much responsibility due to the facility being short-staffed made maintaining good control very challenging. My weight was ballooning, my blood pressure was high, and I was exhausted; but all that still couldn't keep me down. I was so insanely happy to be pregnant, to be growing the life inside me. I still cannot come close to putting words to the feeling.

At five months pregnant, I went on temporary disability due to my difficulty controlling my blood sugars with the added stress of my job. My blood sugars improved, and I became even more elated. My weight gain was rapid, and my high blood pressure continued to climb. Either my memory of this time was poor and the doctors really did advise me to watch my salt intake or perhaps they knew I was a nurse—albeit a very new one—and would know better; but I did not cut back on my salt intake despite a diagnosis of preeclampsia. Preeclampsia is a potentially very dangerous condition for pregnant women resulting in high blood pressure and damage to one or more organs. Left untreated, it could be deadly to myself or the baby. My daily craving for Top Ramen noodles with cheese melted on top did nothing to alleviate the water retention that was quickly covering my knuckles and turning my face into a marshmallow. My feet were terribly swollen and burned so severely that the only relief to be found was by soaking my feet in a tub of ice water at the end of each day and in the last few months multiple times daily. Thanks to my dog Penny who kept eating the ice cubes, the foot bath never stayed cold for long. Yet still, as uncomfortable as it was, I was still ecstatic. My husband Dustin deployed as a US Marine when I was eight months pregnant. I was devastated that he had to leave, but we had the support of our family, and I was determined to be the unflappable Rachel / mother / Marine wife!

At thirty-five weeks, I saw a doctor at Balboa Naval Hospital in San Diego. I resisted his suggestion for full bed rest. He told me if I couldn't stay in bed then to at least remain at home and take it easy. That was a very challenging week; I was, and still am to this day, awful at sitting still. At thirty-six weeks, my mom took me to my weekly checkup. My blood sugars were still relatively well-controlled with frequent visits to the endocrinologist and my determination to have a healthy baby girl, but my blood pressure was dangerously high. The doctor asked me how I would feel about being admitted to the hospital immediately to be induced in the morning. "Great!" I tell them. I've got my bag in the car. (Much to the surprise of my mom, who I suppose I might have given a heads-up about this possibility. Sorry, Mom!)

After being induced, being attached to every cord under the sun, and settling in at the hospital, I was able to contact my handsome Marine, floating somewhere in the middle of the ocean on the USS *Tarawa*. The Red Cross made the connection and first asked my nurse if my life was threatened and if I *needed* my husband here with me. Dumbfounded by the question—*Well, ah, duh, of course I need my husband, ya schmuck*—I stuttered out, "Uh, yes. Of course I want him here!" Thankfully I was able to talk to him before the epidural, which *did not* work by the way, and in increments until finally our little girl Mckayla decided to make her way into the world. Turns out these questions were asked to decide if the military would fly him back to San Diego to be with me during and/or after the delivery. Apparently I wasn't close enough to death to warrant such a service. I'm still a bit bitter about that.

Because Mckayla was born four weeks early, she ended up staying at the hospital for almost a week. I stayed with her, but as I was recovering quickly and determined to stay by her side, I was not sleeping and was simply exhausted. Since she was born early, her bilirubin was high, and she was tinted with a lovely shade of yellow, jaundice. It was heartbreaking to gaze at my baby girl through the glass of the phototherapy tank. She was blindfolded to protect her eyes and attached to cords to monitor her oxygen levels. Her tiny toes were bruised from repeated pokes when they would check her blood. I would wait eagerly to cradle this little seven-pound angel of mine every two hours when, for a glorious fifteen minutes, I would have the opportunity to breastfeed her and bond. Something about this precious time would put me in such a state of contentment and relaxation that I would start to doze with her in my arms, which of course as a new mother was terrifying!

The doctors suggested I head home and get some sleep. I had been pumping, so I had plenty of milk stocked up. Turns out breastfeeding not only burns calories but also drops your blood sugar approximately 50 mg/dL in my case. I learned that the unpleasant way.

On my way home, I stopped by the store. Realizing that my blood sugar was low as evident by a general weakness and a shaky hand, I confusedly wandered to the soda aisle where I was planning to chug a bottle of juice. I managed to amble to the correct aisle and proceeded to have one heck of a seizure, alerting the store staff of my predicament by clearing an entire shelf of its soda and juice bottles with my flailing arms. This time I awoke as the paramedics were wheeling me into the ambulance. Despite my insistence that I was sufficiently recovered, I was taken to the hospital with a bitten tongue, a bump on the head, and a call to my father-in-law. I was mortified. I was not so much embarrassed that I made a scene at the store, but rather by the fact that my husband's family was made aware of my weakness. I have always had an issue with appearing weak.

For the pregnancy of our second child Gavin, I was already exercising daily and in excellent health, so it did not take one year of planning as it did with our first child. My blood sugars were better than ever before. I worked up until a few days before I was induced as planned, two weeks before my due date. We were living in Oklahoma, Small Town, United States. In between nursing house calls, I would pull over in the tall grass and take a fifteen-minute catnap to rejuvenate myself.

The delivery was fast and not nearly as painful as round one. The epidural worked fantastically; the doctor I had been seeing throughout my pregnancy was present for the delivery. She extended a table out from the end of the bed and gently ushered our little boy into the world after only two contractions.

Postdelivery, I was prepared for the drops in blood sugar and suffered no severe hypoglycemia. Short of the crippling stomach-aches that left me curled in a ball for about fifteen minutes after eating throughout the pregnancy, it was pretty smooth sailing. I knew much better what to expect and what to avoid. The best part, my husband was with me every step of the way.

Chapter 3

God in My Bathtub, Jesus in a Cemetery (2012)

Do you not know that you are a temple of God
and that the Spirit of God dwells in you?
—1 Corinthians 3:16 (NKJV)

For as long as I can remember, I had been searching for the certainty that God exists. Of course many people will say that you come to know God with your heart and not your head, but that was never enough for me. I read so many books trying to understand God's existence, but without the proof, I could not have faith.

One day after my daughter was already two years old, I was taking a bubble bath and reading, once again on that inexhaustible quest for irrefutable proof of God's existence, when a particular topic spoke to me. It referred to God being with us through the hardest times. I began to reflect on the more difficult times in my life, at first thinking how silly it was. Shoot, my life was good—no catastrophes, traumatic deaths, severe pain, or suffering. This required a bit of digging. Most of the time, I would scold myself for ever feeling sorry for myself, but this little bubble-filled moment of quietude was *my* moment, so I reflected on my darkest times.

The birth of our first child was one of the most incredible and significant events in my life up to this point. Of course the pain was extremely unpleasant since the epidural would not work, and watching my newborn lay in the phototherapy tank blindfolded was heartbreaking, but what was most painful was being without my husband. I remember after my supportive mom, who had stayed by my side throughout my pregnancy and delivery, left to go home at my insistence the day after my delivery, I sat and stared at the door hoping that any moment Dustin would walk in. As many mothers know I'm sure, after having your baby be a part of you, growing inside of you for nine months, and then taken away to be monitored elsewhere, it's like having a part of your soul taken away against your will. And not having my husband there with me as well made that emptiness inside me seem so much deeper. The open doorway of my hospital room represented not only a vacancy but also a terrible loneliness. Staring at the empty space in my self-imposed solitude, sobs erupted from me in choking gasps as I poured that black emptiness from inside me out into the open. Mercifully, no one came running to my aide. After a few minutes, I collected myself and walked down to the neonatal intensive care unit (NICU) to visit my baby girl. I knew I was strong enough to handle this. My body felt strong, and with each step toward Mckayla, my heart felt stronger too. It wasn't just me that I needed to take care of anymore. Even then I knew all would work out for the best.

So I sat soaking in the tub reflecting on one of my most sorrowful moments and wondered how I felt so strong in that lonely, silent hospital room. How did I know, without a doubt, that our daughter would be okay? Like a slap in the face, I realized it was because *I was never alone!* Immediately tears streamed down my cheeks. I began sobbing like I had years before in that recovery room, and then the sobs turned into relieved laughter. I was never alone. God was with me—no, *inside* me! I had discovered the Holy Spirit at last.

So from then on, I knew God was there with me always. I did not find God in a book or a church. I found God *in me*, in a bathtub.

I didn't yet believe in Jesus. Although I had already believed in a higher power, making the personal connection—that the Holy Spirit lived in me—was less of a leap than believing in Jesus and the miracles He performed. I felt an overwhelming shame over this;

and I hadn't told anyone, save perhaps my husband, at the risk of spurring a torrential downpour of shock and disapproval from our God-fearing, Jesus-loving friends and associates. I went to church to find Jesus. I prayed to God begging to believe. I read still more books that offered scientific proof of Jesus's life and resurrection. But since the proof was based on the Bible, it wasn't enough for me. The Bible might simply be one of the best collective works of fiction, so how could anyone possibly know? It all seemed too fanciful and whimsical, but more importantly, it felt like a book written to regulate the population through lessons and rules.

I wanted so much to believe. I never gave up. Not long into my marriage, my wonderful and very spiritual mother-in-law Dorothy brought up an interesting point. She asked me why I would be so driven to find the truth. Perhaps God was guiding me, encouraging me through my own need to discover the truth. I love that woman. Those words gave me courage and even more motivation to continue my search.

While Dustin was in the Marine Corps, we were stationed in Oceanside, California, at Camp Pendleton. It was important to us that our family go to church—we wanted our kids to learn about God as well as the Christian values and morals. While Dustin was away for work, and the kids were only two and five, I took them to New Song Community Church, a church we frequented and had come to love. It was a nice message, not particularly personal or even really memorable, probably due to the interruption halfway through by my little man who refused to stay in childcare. He has always been a rambunctious kiddo.

On the way home, we had planned to have a picnic on the beach. Due to traffic, I turned out of the right-turn-only driveway, necessitating a U-turn at the next light in order to head back toward the beach. The next light was another left turn only. This took us into the San Luis Rey Mission in Oceanside, California. I figured we'd make the U-turn in the parking lot. Looking around, we agreed this would be a nice place to check out and perhaps have our picnic. The closest entrance brought us into the cemetery. This magnificent piece of history, open to all, was founded in 1798, with graves dating back to the 1800s and beautiful statues erected throughout.

The older portion of the cemetery sat next to the mission with pathways weaving throughout, housing ancient gravestones whose occupant's names were barely legible due to being over two centuries old. A quiet fountain sat serenely trickling in the center. I instructed the kids not to walk on the graves, but to rather stay on the path, and then allowed them to look around. Gavin and I meandered up to a lovely statue standing a few feet taller than me, of Jesus. His arms reached out as if to tell me, "Stop, listen, and learn." The closer we came, the stronger I felt compelled toward the spot. Standing in front of the statue, the light shining behind it casting my small son and I in shadow, I suddenly felt nervous. I felt small. I felt that rock lodged in my throat and chest that told me this was more than a molded lump of concrete. Well, perhaps not, the statue was merely a statue.

However, in that moment, I knew Jesus was there with me. Every sermon I had heard and all the scripture I had studied finally came together like puzzle pieces to form a gloriously vibrant picture. The culmination of His truth welled inside me and burst forth in a relieved, joyous gasp. I smiled as the tears collected in my eyes then streamed freely down my cheeks. I laughed out loud and silently thanked God, then I took my son's tiny hand and we continued our walk through the cemetery while I enjoyed an overwhelming peace at finally knowing in my heart that Jesus was indeed very real.

At last my *aha* moment did not come with the words printed in some scientific book—it came to me in the bright sunshine, with my son at my side, completely unprepared to finally have my prayer answered. I at last knew in my heart Jesus was real and He loves me.

Chapter 4

Emotional Turmoil

*Be anxious for nothing, but in everything by
prayer and supplication, with thanksgiving,
let your requests be known to God.*
—Philippians 6:11 (NKJV)

Looking back approximately ten years to when I began organizing my thoughts to paper, I seemed so emotionally unsteady. My thoughts seemed so chaotic and all-consuming, like I felt that I was treading water, hardly able to keep my head above the waves at times. Coming to know God as I have these past few years, I have noticed all the preoccupying thoughts that seemed so important at the time seem so trivial now. But they were not trivial—they were part of what makes me who I am now. Each moment of unrest is an experience that has taught me to appreciate the peaceful moments that I am now able to enjoy more and more each passing day. Jesus has calmed the tempest of my mind, and He has answered my prayers time and time again.

Tides

My largest subbattle living with diabetes has always been diet, more specifically, with the emotions associated with food. I am an emotional eater. No, that sounds too tame. I am a tempestuous glutton. I have never been grotesquely overweight. In fact, considering my 5'8" big-boned frame, I am probably only about ten pounds overweight; yet in my head, I have been grotesque, unsightly, and a picture of weakness during my darkest moods. If I am exercising daily and eating healthy, my 170 pounds feels just right. I have always had my good days, or months, when I was on the right track; but when I would fall, I fell hard.

That wonderful willpower hits me like a tidal wave. I feel strong, powerful, and unstoppable for days, weeks, and sometimes months. I avoid temptations, feeling more empowered with each refusal. I stare in the mirror feeling excited rather than saddened. My clothes fit better. The weight of the world seems lighter on my shoulders.

Then the waters of willpower recede. What's left behind is the wreckage, the crumbling structure of strength I had worked so hard to build. Slowly my old cravings begin to creep back into my mind, perhaps due to stress, not enough sleep, or missing a few workouts. It doesn't seem to take much for the landslide to start. Panic sets in as I rationalize splurging once a week, then daily, and then all throughout the day.

When the willpower returns, within two to three days of cleaner eating—which particularly means steering clear of high carbohydrates, processed junk food, and of course candy—I am able to cut back on my insulin.

After a trend of higher blood sugars that may last from a couple of days to a couple of months, when my blood sugars are better regulated, it may take some time for those lovely little warning signs to again become as finely tuned as I would like. It's not until I have been over 300 mg/dL for at least an hour that I start to feel ill, and if my sugars were running erratic for too long, I begin feeling low around 85 mg/dL instead of 65 mg/dL as I do when I am at my best.

The most frustrating thing about living with diabetes is feeling hungry when my blood sugar is high and feeling no hunger whatsoever when my blood sugar is low. I despise eating when I am not hungry because the lack of hunger seems like such a rarity! However, I do notice I am less hungry when blood sugars are within normal parameters. When it is high, all I want to do is eat.

Escape Hatch

The second of the twelve steps to recovery through Overeaters Anonymous states, "Come to believe that a Power greater than ourselves could restore us to sanity" (www.oa.org/newcomers/twelve-steps). I strive for sanity. In 2008, I felt I was losing that sanity when I couldn't seem to control my eating and then became overwhelmed by the inevitable depression that followed such episodes, often resulting in hyperglycemia, high blood sugar. It's a cycle, a very frustrating and destructive cycle.

I often looked to that higher power to break the cycle, to reach down and smack me in the face to stop my addiction. I'm sorry to say I'd come to realize it definitely did not work that way. There is good news though. I. Was. Not. Alone. Whether or not one believes in a higher power, there will always be others who are going through similar struggles—diabetes, bulimia, anorexia, overeating, exercise obsession, and depression; no one is perfect.

My best friend since early childhood struggled with the plights of motherhood, working full time and a challenging marriage. She seemed to hold me on this ridiculous pedestal as if I could do no wrong, as if I had no serious problems. What for so long she didn't know was that I was always afraid. My fear was that someone might discover that I was not as strong as I wished to appear. I wanted to be the one others depended on. I wanted to be the rock, the tearstained shoulder, the ear filled with others' safely stored secrets. I didn't want to let anyone into my mess of a head. I felt like there was no one I could share all my troubles with, only different segments of my personality and issues. As I got older and passed the big three-oh, I realized that although my life was more stable as I had hoped, my emotional stability was challenged with more intricate issues. With fewer of the childhood insecurities, I was less concerned with what others thought of me but instead became obsessed with maintaining the ground I had worked so hard to attain. With diet and exercise, for the first time in my life, I was able to look in the mirror and feel happy with my appearance.

After Gavin was born, I continued to suffer the sensitive stomach issues I had throughout my pregnancy. Certain foods would provoke nausea, and eating too much would result in vomiting. The first couple of months postdelivery, I dealt with it, trying to avoid the triggers that caused me to vomit. I never spoke with a physician about the matter because it didn't seem to be a big issue and I was much more concerned with my infant son. I had fantastic willpower to avoid unhealthy foods and was motivated to exercise once or twice daily. I lost the baby weight after five months and continued to lose another ten pounds over the next month. At that time, I weighed less than I could ever recall as an adult, and I felt fabulous!

Then came the stress. The stress of needing to rent out our home, the stress of a military relocation, the stress of taking our children out of their wonderful day care, and then finally the stress of quitting my job to become a stay-at-home mom. With the stress came that old coping mechanism, the dreaded return of my archnemesis, *food*.

Thus began my issues with bulimia. My sensitive stomach still being troublesome, I learned how to trigger the need to vomit. At first all I had to do was eat too much, and then it began to take a little encouragement. Once I figured out a way to induce vomiting, I would only do it maybe once a week. I was sneaky about it, always very careful not to be caught and only when I ate food I knew I shouldn't.

I began to fear for my very young daughter. My whole life I have struggled with food, overeating, binge eating, and now purging. I had always been very controlling over what and when my daughter ate, rarely allowing the boredom snacking that so often comes with youth. I was so very concerned that she would catch me at it, so I finally searched for help.

Somehow I had this bright idea that seeing a counselor would fix all my issues. I guess I hoped he would have some brilliant advice that would offer enlightenment. So after I left the kids with Dustin, explaining I needed to talk to someone about my issues with food, I made the drive. The two most memorable pearls of wisdom I took from the visit was first, he told me I looked great and that I didn't need to lose weight. At first I was flattered, and then it only frustrated me more. I didn't need to hear that I didn't have a problem. I needed to hear the confirmation that I had an issue and what I could do to relieve said issue. My primary concern that provoked the visit, my budding bulimia, was brushed aside to discuss my food obsession. So the second *pearl* was that I should no longer keep a food journal. Okay, I was obsessive. I see that now. The food journal was a waste of time.

I suppose deep inside, the counselor's dismissal made me believe that the purging wasn't so terrible. I'm a nurse for goodness sake. I knew better! But the brain works in mysterious ways. I was also terribly disappointed that there was no miracle cure, no miraculous advice offered by the counselor. I began purging more and more. I became a pro, sneaky and efficient. I learned which foods to avoid since they seemed to remain in my system. I learned how long to wait after eating. I did not lose weight, I gained a bit, but I was satisfied enough that I wasn't gaining more.

Then came my first wake-up call. I began to experience that all-too-familiar feeling of an oral infection, so I had to have a decayed molar pulled. No big deal. I'd had teeth pulled before. I did not smoke, drink alcohol, or use straws. I was actually excited at the prospect of not being able to eat for a day or two. Obsessed much? While it was healing, I still occasionally purged. The area became severely infected, caused pain unlike anything I had experienced before, and took weeks to heal completely. For two days, I was reduced to a whimpering mess with a tearstained face and an ice pack or heating pad seemingly permanently attached to my cheek. This was not right. My purging was wreaking havoc on my blood sugars, causing delayed healing and now damaging my mouth. Something had to change, so I began trying to help myself.

I decided to share my embarrassing secret with my best friend. No judgment, no pity. Thank goodness. Pity from others made me feel extremely uncomfortable. Apparently only I can give it, not receive it. She gave me an ear; it was exactly what I needed. Immediately I felt a few pounds of weight lift off my shoulders. I liked to think maybe sharing this gross imperfection with her may have allowed her to feel like she could relate to me more and wouldn't feel so hesitant to share her issues with me. This was the first step, speaking my problem aloud. The counselor didn't count; I had no intentions of ever returning.

I love my husband more than words could ever express, but aside from my daughter, he was the last person I wanted to know about my smelly little habit. He had enough to be concerned with, preparing for a deployment and working a stressful job. I took pride in keeping the house clean, taking care of the children, and preparing healthy meals. I could not allow for the crack in the veneer of my sanity to show. I wanted to patch it up, leaving the scar invisible to everyone else who didn't already know. I had to tell my mom though. I hate to admit it, but even though I trust and love my mom implicitly, she was frequently the last to know about my issues. I knew she was not fragile. I just hated to worry her, and I dreaded her pity. She has since become one of my greatest confidants. All that said, I told her everything. Yet more weight lifted and I felt somehow cleaner. She has been my sister in food addiction; she understood more than anyone could. If it's possible, I loved her even more for her understanding. Of course she was concerned, more than she let on I'm sure.

With my secret out, and my drive to heal, I was working to mend my bulimia. I understood that my food obsession was my primary concern and that the bulimia was an aftereffect, an easy out. I needed to take responsibility for what I put in my mouth and stop resorting to purging as an escape hatch. I was not perfect and I never would be, but I knew I wanted to be around for a long time to see my children grow and spoil my grandchildren. I didn't want to be blind or legless. It would be a long road to recovery, but I could now see the path. I was on it and determined to get to the end!

When my husband deployed, I was left with a horribly empty feeling that I filled with—you guessed it—food. My children, in all their wonderfulness, were also adjusting to their daddy being gone and were therefore acting out in their own way, thus making me feel my sanity slipping away bit by bit. I turned to reading; it has helped me escape before. I was a fan of science fiction for this very reason; it offered an escape from reality and provided something to look forward to. I learned I needed to steer clear of romances; the last thing I needed to see was a two-hour annoyingly "quirky" love story while my own love story was put on hold. I was becoming more depressed, feeling more lost having my husband so far. Many spouses having gone through deployments would agree this was quite normal at the beginning of the separation. What I would never discuss with my fellow military spouses was how it was affecting my conflict with food. I began purging again, quite frequently, and the emotional derailment caused by all the changes as well as the feelings of failure, it was just too much to take.

Feeling I needed help more than ever, I insisted the kiddos and myself attend church. Right away the message I took home was to make a vow, a small one that would be attainable. So I vowed, for one week, to read the Bible at night—to study it, rather. And almost a week in, just a page or two a night, I was feeling lighter at heart. I was back to dancing in the kitchen with my kiddos and laughing again. The next week, I vowed not to purge. My eating habits were not perfect, but during the day, I felt the runaway train that was my mind, shifting to stay on the tracks.

Baby steps.

Dustin was deployed to Afghanistan for seven months. I was surrounded by good friends and a fantastic support group while on my path to healing. When he returned, I broke down and told him what I had been struggling with for over a year, and he too lifted some of that weight off my shoulders. The two best things I did in my process to take better care of myself were to tell the people I loved what I was going through and to turn to God. It was also the hardest thing I had ever done.

I have now been mostly purge-free for years, and I am comfortable with the skin I live in; in fact I have more respect for my body for what it has accomplished after all that I've put it through. My daughter's picture of what it is to be healthy, judging by the lifestyle she sees her mom lead, is far more important than any size 9 pair of jeans I might squeeze into. I make a very conscious effort not to refer to food as *bad*, but rather as a tool. We discuss the importance of proper nutrition as a family in order to feel great, rather than to *look* great.

A Spoon Full of Crazy

I'd read other people's accounts of depression and came to a point where I began to believe what I was experiencing was not that bad.

I had been on and off antidepressants for years, most recently resuming medication after the birth of my second child. I had lost all the weight from the pregnancy, became incredibly healthy, and then had to plan for a big move. The stress of the move—trying to rent out our house and starting all over—spurred my eating issues, which of course sent me spiraling into a whirlwind of mood swings I had been happy to be free of for so long.

I would sit on my bed, staring out the window, wanting nothing more than to crawl back into bed. Baby Gavin would be napping and my daughter at school, and all I could bring myself to do was to stare out the window; one side of my brain was telling me to get up, to snap out of it, that there was nothing to feel depressed about! The other side of my brain was telling me to sleep, to crawl in a dark hole and hide—hide from family and friends who didn't know the real me. I was frustrated with being such a weakling, feeling wretched about nothing. *Snap out of it!* I would scream at myself in my mind so I would get up. I would fold the laundry, read to my son, play with my daughter, and vacuum the floors. And occasionally the knife I was holding while cutting the vegetables would "slip," cutting my palm, and I would feel some strange sort of relief. I would daydream of cutting myself knowing how sick and absurd it was. Most of the time I would resist the desire because I was able to make the distinction that it was an unhealthy desire, that it would do nothing but lead to questions from others about how I had hurt myself.

I have always had trouble communicating my emotional struggles to others. I had this self-imposed idea that it was my job to be the rock for my family and friends. Silly really. In the end my weaknesses brought me closer to some I hold so dear. So I may not have been too forthcoming with how I was feeling, but I spoke to a doctor and resumed taking antidepressants.

I wonder now if that is what made my depression not really that bad. Maybe the fact that I could drag myself out of bed when every brain cell but one told me to sleep was what made me in a better mental state than I thought. I wasn't depressed. I was just sad. When the kids were younger, occasionally I was so down I could do nothing but take deep breaths and plaster that smile on my face until it started to feel real. Other times I would feel ecstatic, jumping around like a monkey, dancing to music in my head, singing at the top of my lungs, thanking God for every beautiful breath I took and every vividly green leaf that fluttered to the ground. So maybe I'm bipolar. So maybe it really doesn't matter what I am, depressed, bipolar, or totally normal. What is normal? I don't know, and I surely don't need to know.

I am who I am, and more and more, I am becoming at ease with myself.

When the kids were five and eight, I organized a parent group at their school. It was a bit of a flop because I had never done anything like this and didn't exactly have an experienced PTA mom showing me the way. I saw the moms gathered together at events and outside the school and wondered why I couldn't seem to mesh. It never came so naturally to me. I kept thinking, *Someone else should be doing this. What the heck am I doing?* I helped out where I could for two years. I'm not exactly sure when I found the time between the school governing board, the development committee, parenting, and work; but I did it.

The first meeting of the second year was less of a flop than the first year's, and I had come to realize something very important about myself. I was not popular. There, I said it. I was awkward and had a wonderful habit of sticking my foot in my mouth. I was not comfortable chatting it up with other moms because I got a strange anxiety that made me feel totally fake no matter what I said. *It's okay. That's me. It's part of who I am.* I may never be the mom who could chat so effortlessly outside the school, attending parties or social gatherings like it's second nature. Maybe everyone felt like this.

But I knew I was a good person. I knew I was trying to do a little good where I could in this world and in the lives of my children, my family, and all of those who I was in contact with. I wanted to be a positive force, a good influence, a reflection of the gratitude I felt for all the blessings in this life. I might not be a picture of perfect mental stability, but I was determined to make a positive impact, no matter how small or how foolish I looked in the process.

Another mom joined the parent group during year two. She had fantastic ideas and the know-how to make them happen. When the school began to teach ideals that Dustin and I felt had no place being taught at school, I handed the parent group to her, gratefully, and I cut all ties with the school's governing board. It was all too much—I was simply overwhelmed, and it was no longer the right place for our children.

I was learning to accept myself and my quirks, insecurities, and imperfections, as we all should. I was also learning about my limitations.

Childhood Depression

As a teenager, I dabbled in *cutting*. It provided some strange sort of relief from the turmoil and darkness that had taken residence in my mind. I had suffered no significant trauma to sink me into such a state. My family wasn't a picture of stability; I had alcoholic parents. I had an alcoholic biological father, and half sisters and a half brother that I barely knew. I was bullied in school and always very socially awkward. I had a disease that required my constant attention. But I was safe, and I was loved.

When I was fifteen, I landed myself in a mental health hospital after one particular cutting episode—one of which resulted in the small fine scars I can see on my hand as I type. These small scars are precious to me. I can recall how I gave them to myself as if it were yesterday. I never desired to end my life. I just wanted someone to notice I was hurting.

Checking in at Mesa Vista Hospital, with my mom and dad at my side, one of the first questions they asked me was if I thought

I needed to remove my shoelaces. I was dumbfounded. *Why in the world would I need to remove my shoelaces?* My hesitation must have told them I was at risk for hanging myself, so the staff asked that I turn them in. At that moment, I was thinking, *Whoa, I don't belong here.* After one week at the hospital, I felt better. It wasn't the counselors or the group sessions that shed a little sunshine in my inner darkness—it was the friends I made. The day after I got there, my roommate joined me. She was limp and weak, laying in her bed with black charcoal reminisce still on her lips when I came back into my room after lunch. This petite Hispanic girl, two years younger than me, became my best friend. She had overdosed and was given charcoal to induce vomiting and then was immediately taken to the hospital for treatment. I don't recall much of my time spent at Mesa Vista, but I clearly remember me and her dancing the tango with our stuffed animals around our room. Such a spark of light, such a childlike joy amidst such a dark time. And what caused such darkness? Teenage hormones. It's so sad to think of other teenage girls suffering through such emotions, not knowing why.

Prescription to Groove

We all have our fix; an activity that resets our stressful lives back to baseline, bringing a more peaceful state of mind. For some it is running, surfing, or reading; for me it's dancing. During nursing school, while my husband was stationed in Japan for a year, I would go dancing at this little club in San Diego, Margarita Rocks, with the same two good friends once a week. We would stay out often till closing, creating our own little protective triangle on the dance floor warding off anyone trying to enter our space. If the triangle was not effective at keeping unwanted attention away, we would spaz out in the craziest arms flailing, legs kicking dance we could manage until our little space was uninhabitable by any other than us three.

Those few hours were not filled with any cathartic talk or massive amounts of alcohol. We were there to dance till we were dripping with unattractive sweat. This was our fix. I could not explain this to many people, others assuming dancing could only be done with a partner. My wonderful husband, although perhaps not quite understanding my need to vent this way, accepted my desire to go out while he was stuck in Okinawa thousands of miles away. It wasn't until years later when I reunited with my half sister Harmony via Facebook that I met another who shared my passion for movement.

When I began seeking help for depression, I started with a psychiatrist. After what seemed like endless questions and answers ringing like "Have you tried…" and my response, "Yes, and it doesn't help," he asked me what brings me joy, what helps me to relax. Immediately I responded, "Dancing!" So the doc prescribed I dance three times a week minimum. Be that at music festivals or simply while in the kitchen singing songs with the kids, I needed to fit dancing of some sort into my routine as it was obviously so uplifting to me. Gradually my drive to follow the advice faded away, but I certainly did notice when I was happy (or manic), I was a dancing fool. I take great pleasure breaking out in dance to music playing at school functions, festivals, and even in the middle of the grocery store, often resulting in horrified looks from my teenager. I frequently catch myself grooving to a particularly upbeat tempo turning into the crazy lady dancing to her own music, and I think it's fantastic. I don't care if people think I'm working with a few loose screws. If I am happy, I am going to dance dagnabbit!

This was a relatively new realization for me, how much dancing really did and still does mean to me. After my heart scare (more on that later), I realized it had been weeks since I had last done the washing-dishes groove. I began singing along to a cheesy kids' song while rinsing the plates and turned around to make sure the minions were also dancing with me, and it hit me—I was feeling better. I didn't realize how ill I had felt until I felt better. One thing is for certain—nothing makes me appreciate health more than sickness. When I'm sick, I don't dance. When I feel great, prepare to be embarrassed because this momma has her groove back!

Combating Sadness

As an introvert, it baffles me that I too can become lonely. I prefer to stay home and maybe have a couple of friends over for dinner and games every few months, but for the most part, I am quite comfortable in the company of my family. I become anxious at social gatherings and feel terribly awkward meeting with new people.

As I have a history of periodically feeling a confounding emptiness, it does not shock me to feel at times as though I am trudging through thick water with an uncomfortable fog creeping into my thought processes. In between chores and helping the kids with their schoolwork, I occasionally catch myself staring longingly out the window; longing for what, I have no clue. I am happy where I am now, I am madly in love with my husband, and I laugh often with my children. Yet on those *off days*, I might require a one-sided inner dialogue, convincing myself not to simply change back into pj's after my postworkout shower. Luckily, having experienced these seemingly unprovoked waves of flat affect in the past, I also know how to snap myself out of it or at least prevent myself from sinking lower into the state of stalled motivation.

As impossible as it may seem at the time to carry out the most trivial of tasks, completing them will often take the edge off the dullness. Having the slightest sense of accomplishment may help to raise me up out of my mild stupor.

When I catch myself becoming easily irritated, I take deep breaths. At times, realizing the reason I am snapping at the kids for an insignificant discrepancy is due to my feeling off my game; it helps me to check my responses to avoid getting angry.

The more challenging emotion that slows me in my tracks is the feeling of disjointedness. My thoughts can feel scattered and disorganized, which leads to frustration and irritation. This occurs when I pile too many tasks on my plate and feel the need to complete them all immediately. Keeping checklists makes a world of difference and helps me to maintain focus while giving me a sense of accomplishment as I cross off the completed task.

During times like we're in now, when we are experiencing unprecedented events and are forced into seclusion, it may be reassuring to remember that we are not alone. I know there are others confronting fear, anxiety, confusion, apprehension, loneliness, and frustration.

I take comfort in knowing we are not alone and that this chaos will not last forever. We will be stronger as individuals and closer as families, friends, and communities. After every storm, no matter how turbulent, the sun will rise again.

High Blood Sugar Bringing Me Down

There is a direct correlation between my blood sugars and my mood. When I am in a slump, I do far too much guesstimating with carbohydrate/Novolog ratio resulting in more high and lows than are healthy. Some time ago, I noticed occasionally on days when my blood sugar was running high I was particularly sluggish. Being physically fatigued makes total sense since a high blood sugar makes me feel like I have the flu, weak, tired, and nauseous. I have noticed I am also often emotionally down, short-tempered with the kids, and irritable with unorganized thoughts. My focus would be off. What frightened me was the realization that these feelings were not simply in response to feeling awful, but a deeper physical reaction to the hyperglycemia; I am damaging my brain. I know this, but why do I forget that while I'm eating constantly during the day? Why am I able to rationalize that hand full of candy? It is not worth it, I know this, but I do it anyway. An oral fixation perhaps; I have tried to chew gum to satiate the need to eat, but that just ends up with me compulsively chewing one piece after another until the entire package is demolished in less than an hour. Staying busy has become my new best friend, a goal easily attainable as a mom!

The Whirlwind

The best way I can think to explain the crushing and completely overwhelming cascade of thoughts and emotions is a whirlwind. The torrent of fears, stress, pain, and frustration seem to come at me in a jumbled mess, unable to grasp at one idea with enough firm determination to make any productive decisions. One minute I am fuming at some slight I could easily have overlooked at another time, and the next moment I am a crumpled fragile wisp of who I really am, bursting into tears.

These storms come rarely, much less frequently than years past. Medication once helped flatten out the highs and lows, but I'm in a place where I'd rather work through it naturally because I know it will not last forever, sometimes as brief as mere minutes, sometimes days or a week, but rarely more. In the final moments of these torrents, I occasionally have an epiphany, some spark of light like an idea or a new determination that helps to edge me out of the emotional turmoil and into a more rational state all while driving me toward new goals.

Fascinating how the mind works.

The Freedom of Being Antidepressant Free

I can do all things through Him
who strengthens me.
—Philippians 4:13 (NKJV)

Moment of truth—my biggest fear is of losing my mind. And that may stem from feeling emotionally unstable for most of my life. As a young girl, I always felt awkward, out of place. At ten years old when I was diagnosed as an insulin-dependent diabetic, I had one more issue that made me different.

Through adolescence, I struggled more, trying to sift through the whirlwind of emotions, seeking out ways to describe the turmoil, calling out for help through cutting, eventually landing me in a rehabilitation home for a week. I remember envying the girl down the hall who was there for anorexia. I wished I could have that issue. Little did I know at the time that I would fight with a one-year long bout of bulimia after the birth of my second child.

I had muddled through multiple antidepressants over two decades. At one point, I suffered through the most intense withdrawals while switching medications. The doctor told me I didn't need to wean off one before beginning the next, and against my better judgment formed from research, I complied. I remember the vortex of emotions that I felt on occasion, made up of fears, insecurities, guilt, and stress rampaging through my mind almost consistently. I became dizzy to the point of tunnel vision while walking down the street. I felt crippling anxiety. It was the most horrible feeling, emotionally, that I had ever experienced, and it lasted almost a week until I demanded from my doctor a dose to wean off the medication.

I believe one major problem people experience with antidepressants, why some people are quick to claim they do not work, is that once a medication begins to do its job, the taker quits taking it. Then lo and behold, the symptoms return. I was guilty of this myself. I was conflicted with not knowing whether my feelings were a result of the medication or of my true personality. Even with the medication, I felt myself experiencing the ups and downs, which I now contribute to being mildly bipolar. Now was this really me or a side effect of the medication—a question I would ask myself for years while on different medications.

When my husband discovered I was taking antidepressants—something I was not intentionally hiding from him, but had not exactly been chatty about—the possible side effects worried him. Out of love and respect for him and my own curiosity, I weaned off them completely. What I discovered was a freedom I had never anticipated, not freedom from the ups and downs or the seemingly irrational sadness (those feelings still occurred to varying degrees), but the freedom of knowing these thoughts and feelings were 100 percent me. Every blank stare out the window while trying to drag myself out of bed, every spastic dance with the thrill of being out in the rain, every momentary lapse into flat affect or irrational anxiety about something trivial, it was all me.

In the past few years, I have come to respect these challenges. I am honest with my husband when I am having a rough few days and allow myself some time to partake in simple things I enjoy like coloring with the kids or writing a blog. Oh wow, writing has been so cathartic! I love the highs, the spurts of energy that have me racing around the house cleaning, sprinting at full tilt until I am bent over wheezing in exhaustion. Most importantly, I have learned to be more patient with myself.

I understand the severity of some people's mental infirmity requires medication, but I am unbelievably grateful to discover that I do not need them anymore. Knowing God and the peace that comes with that relationship, my moods have stabilized significantly. My stressors that once seemed so insurmountable, I can now manage with prayer, patience, and of course trial and error.

The Power of Motion

There is far too little emphasis put on the power of exercise to improve mood and overall health rather than resorting to medication alone. I have discovered exercise to be incredibly restorative and crucial to my mental health. When I am in a state of feeling the *need* to exercise daily, all the other psychological clutter seems more distant. Still, occasionally I have flare-ups of the feeling of absence, blankness that usually do not last more than a day.

These funks like to linger at times. When it's a challenge to get moving, exercise is the last thing on my mind. Of course all the experts will tell you one of the best cures for a lame mood is to get out and get some exercise. Easier said than done. Needing to *get ready* to exercise is sometimes enough of a deterrent, so I will engage in activities that do not require any preparation.

One session is all it takes to uplift my mind solely with the sense of accomplishment after completing exercise. *It's better than if I did nothing at all*, I will tell myself, and it's true. Sometimes, all it takes is something small to move toward feeling better.

Here are my go-to moves when I need to get the blood flowing, but the idea of leaving the house and going for a run seems as likely as a trip to the moon.

1. Doorway push-ups. With my feet about two feet out behind me and hands even with my shoulders. It works the chest and shoulders with minimal impact. I shoot for two sets of ten.

2. Squats. Three sets of twenty, with legs together, hip distance apart, and in plie squat. Again, low impact and it works the inner and outer thighs.
3. Bicycle crunches. Set of twenty sitting up in a V rather than laying on the floor in a traditional crunch; this seems less stressful to the low back and neck.
4. Stretching in between each move, trying to reach every body part.
5. Going for a walk. Even if it's only for ten minutes, it's fresh air!

These moves raise my heartbeat without drenching me in sweat and always result in a lift in my mood, however slight. I set a timer and try to go for longer the next time, and I add moves to target other muscle groups such as leg lifts and wacky jacks if I'm feeling it. I may not win any triathlons with these moves, but every little bit counts, and it's better than if I did nothing at all!

Major Health Scares

*For I consider that the sufferings of this
present time are not worthy to be compared
with the glory that shall be revealed in us.*
—Romans 8:18 (NKJV)

Now looking at forty years old, I am feeling the effects of my imperfect blood sugar control more and more. Of course, no two diabetics suffer the same exact side effects, but I seem to experience very odd symptoms. For many years, I have felt very lucky to not have suffered more severe consequences due to diabetes. I have my eyesight, ten fingers, ten toes, and good kidney function. My one constant companion is peripheral neuropathy, probably one of the most common ailments of diabetics, damage to the nerves in my feet resulting in burning, tingling, and pain.

After living through the following maladies, I have come to believe God has greater plans for me that require me to be in one piece, to share my experiences and for me to be able to relate to other people's illnesses in order to teach, understand, and comfort.

Heart Attack at Thirty-Four?

In 2014, Dustin left the Marines, and we moved to Hawaii to become homesteaders and start a new life away from all the busyness of the city. We moved onto my brother and sister-in-law's huge undeveloped property with plans to purchase some of their land and build our home. For two years, we camped out under an enormous open roof. Dustin built a large platform with an outdoor kitchen onto which we lived out of a small pop-up trailer, a military tent, a freestanding room for the kids, and a bathroom on a trailer. The road up to the property was rough enough to keep any strangers from wandering in, and the surrounding guava and koa forests were wild and beautiful.

As picturesque as the setting was, our situation was fraught with challenges. "It's like we're running up a hill," I explained to my mom one day. "And God keeps throwing rocks at us, driving us back!" Dustin was working hard running his own company to provide for our family. He and I were constantly having car troubles and could never catch up financially, even though we were not paying rent. I was constantly experiencing health issues. The near continuous rain was frustrating given that the wind would blow it right into our outdoor "house." Rats, centipedes, slugs, wasps, spiders, and water damage to pretty much all of our belongings were a constant battle; and all this while trying to work full time and keeping the kids happy, healthy, and educated. Trying to keep some semblance of normalcy became too much to handle. It felt like a test I felt I was failing.

It turns out building a home in Hawaii can be a nightmare. There are so many tedious rules, regulations, and troublesome building permit requirements; it's as if they do not want people to establish themselves on the island. Dustin and I were so stressed we were forgetting to be a team.

While living in this situation, in 2016, I discovered a new diabetes-related issue I had no idea of until I experienced it myself. It all started with a shooting pain in the left side of my chest. *Gas pains,* I told myself. But deep inside, I was wondering if it could be something bigger. I was a working mom with just enough health issues to rationalize ignoring them all.

The pain kept returning, not always on the left side of my chest. At one point, about two months after the initial pain, while reaching up to hang laundry out on the line, the sudden sharp pain shooting from the left side of my chest under my arm, across to the right side, was severe enough to catch my breath and leave me shaken and clutching my chest. It lasted only a second, but it was intense. As the weeks flew by, as weeks tend to fly when you're running around like a chicken with your head cut off, the shooting pains would occur more often causing my breath to catch. Was the breathlessness a symptom associated with the pain or simply due to the psychological effect of the sudden pains, I was not sure. But one thing was for sure, the pains were coming more frequently, at times three to four times a week and other times once every two weeks or so. I began feeling nauseous with these instances as well.

During this time, I was busy as always. I was trying to become more involved with the kids' public charter school, making plans to begin a parent organization similar to a PTA, continuing to be a member of the governing board, and taking on more hours at work. I was still trying to watch my weight, eat healthy, and exercise daily.

Finally I got my wake-up slap in the face. I decided to go for a run down the gravel road by our house. I had been tired that day and the last two days before, but I got a break, a brief responsibility-less moment for some calorie burning me time. On my way down, 1.5 miles on a steep decline, my chest was aching, and my breathing seemed more challenging than usual. At the bottom, I stopped to stretch, breathe, and get ready for the way up. I was tired! I quickly realized running up that hill was not in the cards. My heart was racing, and I was exhausted, so I kept a brisk pace. I could not seem to find my breath, even when I stopped. I was so breathless my chest was becoming tight, and there was a pressure and ache in my chest stronger than ever before. I was nauseous and dizzy, really dizzy. Somehow I made it up the hill, more afraid than in pain. After a shower and a rest, the pain was dissipating, but the nausea and dizziness were pretty awful. I was unable to sleep that night due to feeling like my heart was trying to jump out of my chest. Two glasses of wine seemed to calm my anxiety.

The next day, I sat in the cardiologist's office, the last appointment of the day so that I would still be able to work a full day. The electrocardiogram (EKG), a test in which electrodes are attached to your chest, arms, and legs to measure electrical activity in the heart, did not show anything of significant concern other than an occasional skipped beat. The doctor offered nitroglycerin for the mild chest pain I was currently feeling right there in the office. He informed me that if the nitro relieved the pain, it would indicate this was related to my heart. The nitro did relieve the pain, almost immediately. Only a few minutes later, I felt a rush of heat to my head with a dull headache, but the chest pain was gone. "Oh, well, this can also indicate heartburn or indigestion," the doc tells me. So he gave me a prescription for omeprazole to begin daily to test if the pain was due to heartburn or chest pain and planned to schedule another appointment to set up for a twenty-four-hour heart rate monitor. As I stood up to leave, a wave of dizziness hit me hard bringing me too close to what it must feel like to blackout. For the first time, I experienced tunnel vision, and the lights dimmed in my line of vision as I swayed against the doorjamb. Understandably the doctor was concerned and stated he would feel much better if I went to the ER for more testing. I assured him I was okay, and then after taking a few steps and nearly falling into the wall, I agreed with the good doctor as he insisted his nurse give me a ride to the ER conveniently located less than a mile away. *Nonsense!* "I can drive," I insisted. Wow, I was stubborn. So I compromised to allow the nurse to accompany me in my car with another nurse following behind to give her a ride back. This way, I would have my car with me at the ER. Looking back, I see this was a little selfish. I do not like to appear weak; I could drive down the street dagnabbit.

At the ER, there were questions, questions, and more questions and heart, oxygen, and blood pressure monitors. My oxygen saturation was good; I didn't smoke, so when the nurse put the supplemental oxygen nasal cannula on my face, I asked why. Okay, so I get why now, but at the time I did not want any extra attachments. The nurse gave me a baby talk condescending response to which I broke out the "I'm a nurse" card to get a little respect. Okay, I'm a little young for a heart attack lady, but not so young that you need to talk to me like an idiot. Other than that, the staff at the ER were courteous and kind. The EKG (yes, another one) revealed nothing significant (yeah, nor did the one done thirty minutes ago). But the chest pain, although improved, was real, and the pressure was consistent.

The doctor recommended I be flown to a specialist in Oahu. *Hmm, an adventure, an experience, oh yeah, and possible answers. Okay, let's do this.* After a phone call with the husband and my sister-in-law the doctor, I was prepped for flight. *Oh, wait. What? No helicopter. Sigh.* On the plane, or rather the people/cargo puddle jumper, I experienced morphine for the first time. The life flight tech wanted me at a pain level of 0/10. One dose of morphine did not do the trick, nor did the second. By the third, even the chest pressure was hardly noticeable, no pain whatsoever. I was being lulled to a stoned state by the hum of the plane, and the occasional blood pressure cuff puffing up even felt relaxing. Oh, if I only knew what that morphine would do to me—or maybe it was the nitro—but I'd rather have had the chest pain.

In the hospital, I was admitted for the night in order to run tests—more morphine, supplemental oxygen, and explanations of what testing we would be doing. Depending on the next few hours, I would possibly need an angiogram, an x-ray of the coronary arteries after dye is injected into the blood in order to look for narrowing or blockages in the major blood vessels. Little Waimea, Big Island Hawaii, did not have that technology.

Once I was settled in my hospital room, a cozy, quiet room with a lovely view of a wall and a TV, an overwhelming sense of peace came over me. I was in a place where I could get answers; in the early hours of the morning, I might now catch a catnap. As a mother / nurse / cook / teacher / dog walker, washer and trainer / chauffeur / wife / maid, it seemed I had to escape to the hospital to get a few moments of peace where I didn't feel the overwhelming urge to leap up and fold laundry or document on last week's nurse visits. So yes, in this cozy little shared hospital room on an island not my own, I was very content.

Another EKG (I was going to be sticky tomorrow) and a quick snooze (very quick), the doc walked in, young, with a smile and a light step. He pulled up a chair, sat, and proceeded to tell me I couldn't possibly be having a heart attack. He told me he was planning on seeing something other than the young healthy woman he saw in front of him. *Oh, gee thanks, Doc.* I could have been flattered. I was not flattered. I was frustrated. I frequently have health issues that pop up that either get ignored by me or, if I do take the time to address, they vanish by the time I get in to see someone about it or there is no identifiable cause. So after all I had experienced in the last eight hours, to have another doctor tell me I was too young and fit (uh-huh) to be having heart problems, I was ready to jump off that comfy little bed and smack that smile off his prepubescent face. But I was non-confrontational until the end, so I smiled and awkwardly thanked him for his misplaced compliment. *Schmuck.*

So since the EKG was not showing anything to be concerned about (seeing a trend here?), the little cardiologist wanted to run a stress test. Hours later and after a couple of doses of morphine for the chest pressure, the nitro patch was removed from my chest due to the dull headache that seemed to be gradually ramping up. I was told we would be doing the stress test in the next hour. I was incredibly weak by this point, nauseous, and dizzy, which I attributed to the lack of sleep (well, duh, what was I expecting at a hospital?) and food. When I took my first few steps, I was overcome by exhaustion. My attempts to be friendly and cheerful, to make people smile, were swiftly going out the door as I nearly lost yesterday's stomach contents all over the floor. I kept my cool and made it to the wheelchair. The room they took me to was cramped, space enough for the treadmill, hospital bed, and a few monitors. Little doc had returned along with a tech that hooked me up with more electrodes (yay!) for another EKG. On the treadmill while holding on for dear life, by some miracle, I was able to run (sans sports bra; oh, good Lord) while holding the wires and got my heart rate up to 150 bpm. At around 120 bpm, I felt a catch in my chest that took my breath and made me feel like my chest was momentarily hollow. "Oh, that," the doc said. "That was just a skipped beat." *Ohhh, just a skipped beat, nothing to be concerned about.* Well, from my point of view, it was something to be concerned about. Me, who has had a regular heart rate my entire life, felt that skipped beat and thought I might drop off the treadmill.

Maybe small potatoes to you, Doc, but I was feeling like a big 'o pot of mashed spuds!

I survived the stress test with no obvious causes for concern, so therefore no need for an angiogram due to the potential complications of blood vessel damage and an allergic reaction to the dye used. I was taken back to my room with plans for an ultrasound and then possible discharge if there were no other concerns.

This is when I experienced, what I will call from here on out, the migraine from hell. Back in bed and incredibly weak, my head began to throb, my eyeballs hurt, and my ears hurt. I curled into a ball and vomited. When I called the nurse, she gave me ibuprofen, which did nothing, but ice did help. I believe I may have lost consciousness during the cardiac ultrasound due to the pain. I'm not sure but I felt like I was there for hours. Finally, the pain began to dissipate after an hour, maybe two. Shoot, it could have been three. With the pain, the fogginess, nausea, and dizziness also faded significantly. I got up, got dressed, chatted with the nurses, and felt like a new woman. Nothing like feeling enough pain to make you lose consciousness, to make you appreciate feeling somewhat normal again. So I suppose I could thank the morphine or nitro for that. I'm leaning toward morphine for the cause. No worries about this girl getting hooked on that crud in the future! I flew home that night on Hawaiian airlines.

After I had returned home, I met with the cardiologist again. The twenty-four-hour heart rate monitor revealed much the same, skipped beats and, alas, my heart rate dropping into the forties, correlating with the feeling of weakness and dizziness. Okay, that's something, but it still wasn't a diagnosis.

Good ol' internet. A little research fueled my desire to go a different route, dysautonomic syndrome. It was the only diagnosis that seemed to put all the pieces together. It's a term rather than a diagnosis, but it was a start, and I had many of the symptoms described associated with this issue. I brought the term to a neurologist who agreed with me and narrowed it down further to autonomic neuropathy. Autonomic neuropathy refers to symptoms that occur when the nerves that control the involuntary functions that your body perform normally on a daily basis such as digestion, blood pressure, heart rate, and bladder function are damaged and not receiving the messages from your brain properly.

According to Mayoclinic,

> Autonomic neuropathy occurs when the nerves that control involuntary bodily functions are damaged. This may affect blood pressure, temperature control, digestion, bladder function and even sexual function. The nerve damage interferes with the messages sent between the brain and other organs and areas of the autonomic nervous system, such as the heart, blood vessels and sweat glands. While diabetes is generally the most common cause of autonomic neuropathy, other health conditions—even an infection—may be to blame. Some medications also may cause nerve damage. Symptoms and treatment will vary based on which nerves are damaged. (http://www.mayoclinic.org/diseases-conditions/autonomic-neuropathy/basics/definition/con-20029053)

To this day, when I am stressed or overly tired, my body will often let me know before I realize it myself. I will feel fatigued and my heart will start skipping beats, and I will catch myself holding my breath. Deep breathing, gentle exercise, and being sure to get enough sleep usually relieve the symptoms within a day or two.

Seizing the Moment: Another Wake-Up Call

For some reason, maybe it's part of my pesky human nature, my glorious health-related epiphanies are all too short-lived.

My erratic heart rate and halting breaths taught me a very valuable lesson—slow down, cut back on stress, exercise, and eat well. I slowed down and trimmed back my obligations that had me stretched too thin. I got some sleep and cleaned up my diet. I got back into a fitness routine.

Then like how a trickling stream from a rainstorm begins to cut a rivet in the soil, I begin collecting more responsibilities, taking on more tasks, again stretching myself too thin. I wanted to work more; I loved my job, so why not earn more money at it? I wanted to be more present at the kids' school; parents should be more involved. Hey, somebody's got to organize it! I wanted to start cultivating our land so we could feed our family. I wanted to train our dogs. I wanted to keep a spotless living space. Okay, those last three were more of a fantasy given our living situation at the time, but that didn't stop me from thinking about it all night when I should be sleeping.

So it turns out I *might* be a bit compulsive. And apparently when I am packing more of my time with obligations, I *might* feel the need to let loose—compulsively drinking?

Thanksgiving 2013 came along and I was off call at work for the first time in a week. In fact, I had two whole days off, no on-call, no nurse visits, no running to and back from school, no meetings. Two glorious days of cooking, cleaning, and family time. So I drank some wine and then some adult eggnog (I know, brilliant for a diabetic), and then straight for the hard stuff, more and more whiskey added to the eggnog. This was a family dinner we're talking about. I way overdid it. Although embarrassing, that wasn't the slap in the face. The seizure the next morning I suffered from due to not waking up in time to take glucose was not the wake-up call either. The reaction to the glucagon was the dive into frozen water, the shove out of the plane, the slap in the face I needed.

Glucagon injections—the rescue shot intended to quickly raise blood glucose, ending hypoglycemic convulsions, that is, the seizure—had always given me a hangover of sorts, contributing to one of my very first migraines as a preteen. Little did I know in those early years that migraines and I would be good friends. I was never truly sure whether the headaches were a side effect of the glucagon or a lasting effect of the seizure, until my husband was deployed and I experienced my first solo seizure. I had awoken in the middle of the night thanks to my subconscious-delivered wake-up dream, a dream in which there was a king and queen seated upon a throne up above me, and immediately recognized the signs of low blood glucose. As the symptoms of a low blood sugar typically build slowly when I'm awake, the experience is usually more startling when waking from a sound sleep, a metallic taste in my mouth, heart racing, panic, and a sense of urgency. On this night, I awoke with these symptoms, ate a granola bar, and went back to sleep. The details are a bit of a haze now as I recall, which only reinforces the idea that it was indeed a seizure. So fast-forward about two or three hours, and I awoke with a wet bed and a very sore jaw. No, the baby was in her crib. I couldn't blame the wet bed on her, and was that the taste of blood in my mouth? Ooooh, great. So, yeah, did I mention during a seizure, or at least my experience with them, all your muscles contract including your bladder? Oh, the joys of diabetes. Short story long, no headache, no nausea or weakness other than the usual muscle fatigue from trying to run a marathon while unconscious. So it is clear to me my system accepts the message to deliver sugar into my bloodstream the glucagon demands, but it does not appreciate it. Apparently my snack was not eaten soon enough to stop the seizure, but must have brought my glucose up eventually.

The morning after Thanksgiving 2016, I woke at six forty-five for my Lantus shot, drank some water feeling fine (not dreadfully hungover), and fell back to sleep. At about eight o'clock, my heart racing out of my chest woke me, and I jumped out of bed to find the glucose. Getting it from where I thought it was on top of the fridge in a box, I started to feel it was too late as evidenced by my neck muscles tightening and that disjointed feeling of pending doom and called Dustin just in case, as I had many times before. He was all too familiar with this drill; although in over twenty years he had only given me glucagon a couple of times, we have done the "just in case, get it ready" dance many times. Part of this drill included me sitting on the floor so that I didn't fall face first and break another front tooth as I did as a teenager during a seizure in the bathroom. Ah, memories. The last thing I remember before coming back to myself sitting at the kitchen table was confusedly pointing in the wrong direction to where the glucagon was.

It was then as I crawled back into bed hunched over in pain an hour later that I prayed a prayer I thought I never would. *God, get me through this, and I will change.* The diarrhea, nausea, vomiting, migraine, and body pain—it was all too much, packed into this body that had been so strong for me, now left trembling, limp, and useless. I knew it was not the alcohol. It was a reaction to the glucagon, and as I got older, my reactions were getting worse as was my sensitivity to the glucagon. More importantly, I stood by my belief that events in life happened for a reason. I got a message, a painful one, that left my brain in a fog for two days after, one that left me weak and sick, unable to get out of bed for hours that felt like years. For a moment, I saw very clearly, my purpose renewed—share my story, help others. And I could not do that if I was dead. Alcohol had gotten in the way of that purpose, so it had to go. Knowing this crutch I leaned on to help me relax had now been thrown into the fire, I felt a great weight lifted off my shoulders. For the first time since I kicked the binging habit, I felt released from the grip of a damaging addiction. I felt free. Oh yes, I was compulsive by nature, and knowing that would keep me stronger.

Since those proclamations to myself, determining not to drink, I have resumed and then quit again. Whenever I felt like I was at a point of *needing* a drink, I knew it was time to take a break. Coming from a line of alcoholics, and having alcohol contribute so significantly to the loss of both my stepdad and my biological father, I knew I needed to tread very cautiously. Addiction was in my blood.

Now I have been alcohol free for over a year. I miss it. I miss the relaxation that comes with a glass of wine or two after a long, stressful day. However, I certainly do not miss the feeling of not being in control.

Cramping My Style

Jumping back in time to 2001, I was working in a warehouse stocking pallets with clothing while sporadically attending junior college classes still trying to figure out what to do with my life. I had always been a big-boned girl with a muscular upper body and

46

enjoyed physical work, so I began attending classes toward becoming a firefighter.

I began experiencing cramping first in one hand and then the other followed by tingling in my fingertips and difficulty grasping objects. After meeting with a doctor and being moved to a position at work that would not be placing my hands and arms under repetitive strain, I became familiar with the pain that can be associated with carpal tunnel syndrome. The shooting pains darting up to my elbows would prevent me from reaching out to grasp objects, and the cramping in my wrists and the feeling of pins and needles in my fingers would keep me awake at night. I attended occupational therapy and performed the recommended stretches and exercises before finally deciding to have carpal tunnel release surgery.

The surgery went well. The recovery was uncomfortable but immediately relieved my symptoms, and I responded well to occupational therapy. The surgeon informed me he had removed significant scar tissue that was most likely made worse due to my diabetes, and I might need to reconsider my career choices. While attending occupational therapy, I was lucky to meet the wonderful people who helped steer my mind in a new direction for my future, health care. I began working as an occupational therapy heath aid with the very people whose patience and skill helped me to recover from a physically painful situation.

During this time, my stepdad's mother suffered partial paralysis following a routine epidural for back pain. I began to help care for her since she was no longer able to walk, eventually moving in with her. I came to realize I enjoyed helping to care for people, and the less than glamorous aspects that come with caregiving such as wound care were not upsetting to me. Again I was blessed by the people in my life and had the opportunity to know a few nurses including my dad's awesome new wife. After speaking with them, I began to pursue an education in nursing, a career I now love and am grateful to have every day of my life. Who knew carpal tunnel syndrome could be such a blessing? God always has a plan.

Sudden Seizures

Living with type 1 diabetes, I have become very accustomed to health issues. As I age, common viruses hit me harder and harder each time. Blood sugar fluctuations leave me feeling like I have the flu or have me sweating with shaking hands and a sense of dread. But the fatigue I had complained of for years, which was simply brushed off as being due to the stressors of a working mom, was getting suddenly worse. I was also becoming dizzy and sweating profusely at night.

As an on-call nurse, I frequently took call in the middle of the night, so when my fatigue became concerning, my husband's first idea was that my sleep was so disrupted that I was not getting enough rest. At the time we were providing respite care for a sweet little one-year-old boy, so he woke me up once or twice a night. I was also using the insulin pump at the time, so I would be awoken with the alarms of low/high blood sugars as well as the notifications to verify my blood sugar to check that my continuous glucose monitor was working properly. I have never liked to take time off work because I hate for other people to need to pick up my slack, so I had plenty of sick and vacation time stored up. When I took one week off to get some uninterrupted rest and my fatigue seemed no better, the doctor advised I wean off the Cymbalta (duloxetine) I was taking for my peripheral neuropathy, thinking my symptoms may be due to side effects of the medication. When I called soon after to report my occasional forgetfulness was also worsening, he advised me to stop the Cymbalta completely. Well, this resulted in some lovely withdrawal symptoms, but I got through that nasty week with no improvement to my symptoms.

It got serious when my vision changed. I can best describe it as an old-fashioned movie reel flashing slides behind my closed eyes. With my eyes open, I was seeing shadows. My already sensitive ears became even more fragile as any loud noise made me flinch. The day after my vision changes began, while walking around the store with my kids, I began shaking. I had to sit down and take deep breaths till I felt secure enough to walk, but I was notably disoriented.

My experience at the store convinced me to get into the doctor as soon as possible that same day, two hours earlier than my already scheduled appointment. I became convinced what I was experiencing was seizure activity and decided to go to the emergency room with hopes of getting some testing. At the ER, they conducted a spinal puncture at my request and a computerized tomography scan (CT). The intensity of the sound and effort to keep still seemed to be enough to provoke my first real nondiabetes-related seizure. After the techs rolled me out of the scan, every muscle in my body tensed; and I began shaking such small yet intense tremors that when the nurse asked me, "Are you okay? Are you cold?" with a very concerned look on her face, all I could mutter was, "Mmmmmy mmmmmu…" I was trying to say my muscles were what…shaking? Tense? The tremors only lasted about a minute.

The spinal puncture was intensely painful and incredibly nauseating. In a hospital gown, I was positioned sitting on the side of the bed facing the wall, hunched over a bed side table with my torso in a C-curve exposing my back. The area was numbed with spray prior to the long, thin needle being inserted between two lumbar vertebrae in order to withdraw cerebrospinal fluid. I can only fathom how unbearable it would have been without the topical numbing agent applied. The needle being inserted felt like a thin hot spear being slowly forced into my spine. The pain was so intense, and I felt a wave of nausea within seconds. I discovered pain provoked my tremors as I struggled to keep as still as possible with the lance pierced into my spinal column. I have had two epidurals with childbirth, but somehow this was a whole new ball game of pain given my fearful state of mind. I requested the procedure be done to rule out multiple sclerosis and infections such as meningitis or encephalitis as the cause of what I now thought to be seizures.

My CT scan came back normal. They discharged me from the ER quickly, deciding not to conduct the MRI as they had originally planned. They stated they were able to rule out stroke or anything life-threatening. The doctor shared no thoughts on my tremors, confusion, shadowed vision, or weakness. After almost daily calls from me to the ER and my primary care doctor, one week later, I received the results from my spinal puncture—I had bands in my blood and cerebrospinal fluid, immature white blood cells that can occur in response to infection, inflammation in the spinal cord, and who knows what else. Inconclusive.

I was referred to a neurologist to discover what was going on. The neurologist conducted a sleep study and an electroencephalogram (EEG). The EEG consisted of electrodes placed on my scalp to monitor my brain activity while I was asked to answer math equations, which at the time was a joke. I could not focus on anything. Although, during the hour-long test, I was shaky and seeing flashing lights every time I closed my eyes, the test did not reveal any significantly concerning brain activity.

I also flew to Oahu to have a brain MRI done. I was fearful that being confined to a small space would spur another episode of tremors. I came to dread those moments. The facility was beautiful and calming with soothing lighting and large fish tanks. The procedure provoked only a slight tremor but quickly faded within minutes, leaving me feeling slightly weakened but otherwise myself.

After months of waiting for referrals, results, testing, talking to doctors, time off work, and lots of prayers, I finally got an answer, "We don't know what is causing your symptoms."

Thanks to the spinal puncture, blood work, CT scan, and brain MRI, I knew what it wasn't, most likely. It wasn't multiple sclerosis (which at one point I was convinced that it was), and there were no brain tumors or evidence of seizure causing scar tissue or damage. Other than bands present in my blood and cerebrospinal fluid and an elevated A1C, my blood work was normal. My sleep study revealed I had sleep apnea, and the DEEG revealed I have healthy brain tissue. I felt very lucky to have had most of these tests come back normal. But at the moment it was twisted; I'd rather have a serious diagnosis to plan treatment for and know the cause of my symptoms than to know all that was *not* wrong.

Depending on the day, stress, pain, certain sounds, and flashing/flickering lights seemed to trigger an aura, or the feeling you get before having a seizure, which would eventually turn into full-body tremors and involuntary muscle jerking. I can best explain it as an electrical storm coursing through my entire body, often most severe in my shoulders, arms, neck, and head. I would not lose consciousness like I do when I suffer diabetic hypoglycemic seizures. I would remain alert. Most times I would develop a stutter and halted speech. Occasionally I'd experience nausea immediately after and always feel fatigued for the rest of the day and sometimes the next day as well.

I had good days and bad days. I'd feel productive for a couple of days, although always tired. I would run errands, shuttle the kids around, and finish yard work. Then the next day I would be wiped out, shaky, fuzzy-minded, startling at the slightest sound, getting chills that would run from head to foot leaving me feeling weakened, and needing to lay down after the most menial of tasks. Just odd.

"What we know," said the neurologist, "is that you have diabetes and sleep apnea, so get those under control." He told me to sleep sitting straight up or on my stomach since I was not quite ready for the C-PAP, to better control my blood sugars, and see what happens. So that was the plan while looking into another career that would allow for me to foster and homeschool.

During this period, I experienced a couple of instances when I thought I might be dying. The uncertainty of my condition—wondering what could be causing my "seizures," weakness, fatigue, and confusion—had me prioritizing my responsibilities should today or tomorrow be my last day. I asked God for just a little more time to get these last couple of things taken care of so that my husband and children were not left in the dark about anything important. I was fearful at times, but I had a strange sense of peace knowing that if God wanted me, I was ready, *almost.* I felt like I simply needed to finish a couple of tasks first.

As my symptoms slowly eased up, I found myself having more good days, days when I felt like I could function almost normally. I was realizing how important it was not to spread myself too thin. It's human nature to want to feel valuable, needed, like a contributor to our community and family, but not at the detriment of my own health. My 5'8" broad-shouldered self is more frail than it appears, more fragile than I wish it was. With that acceptance, I knew I also needed to be honest with people. I need to be able to say, "No, I'm sorry, but I cannot help." I need to realize that being sick does not make me weak, well, not emotionally or mentally at least.

As these symptoms have now resolved, I developed a few ideas since I never received any definitive cause. Possibly it was related to neuropathy, as if my central nervous system had decided to go on the fritz. I was diagnosed with autonomic neuropathy years ago, so it's certainly not unrealistic, although my endocrinologist was not so sure. I explored the possibility of it being psychological. The most likely cause was the lack of sleep. I had been on call at night for five nights a week for work for almost two years, at times seeing patients during holidays, weekends, and weekdays as well. I had developed the habit of waking at the slightest sound. I would even wake up imagining I had heard my phone ringing or dreading I had missed a call. I believe my sleeping state was only half asleep, never really getting into the restful stage. The lack of rest accumulated to a point where all aspects of my health were affected, memory loss, confusion, weakness, seizures, and *fear for my life*.

The humbling part in all this was that I realized how many truly wonderful, understanding people I have in my life, friends, family, and our church family, who are all too eager to lend a helping hand when they learned I'd been sick. That is a huge blessing, and I will never forget it.

An Angel on My Shoulder

When the surf warning says, "Dangerous shorebreak," it's not a joke.

I consider myself a strong swimmer, so when I heard the announcement on the radio about dangerous swells in January 2021, I didn't exactly ignore it, but the waves looked so small! I'm not the mom that coddles her kiddos, and I prefer to goof off too. I climb trees, skateboard and Rollerblade, jump on the rocks, surf, and play in the rough waves. I have always felt life is too short to let fear of a broken bone stop you from adventuring.

With my dear friend Raine visiting from out of town and our swim with the manta rays cancelled due to poor water visibility, we changed plans last minute to check out my favorite beach. When we got there, the skies were clearing, and the waves, although choppy, were relatively small.

Since we left all the toys at home (bodyboards, surfboards, etc.), we jumped in to play in the waves. Every once in a while, a wave formed that was almost big enough to body surf. A big beauty started to form, and my daughter and I swam hard to catch it; she missed it, but I caught it, and it was powerful enough to carry my body as if it were afloat a board. It was a great ride until it drove me headfirst into the beach, that terrific current jerking my body backward over my head. I heard the pop of my bone breaking.

I crawled forward calling for my daughter to pull me out. As another wave knocked us forward, she tugged on my arm as I slowly rose to standing. My friend rushed over, and they both supported me up the beach away from the waves. *I should not be walking*, was my first thought. My second thought, this one I voiced, was, *There was an angel on my shoulder*.

Instincts must have kicked in because I knew not to move my neck. A slight tremor took hold of my body as the shock of what had just happened struck me like lightning and tears filled my eyes. "God still has plans for me" and "I should not be walking" were the thoughts running in a loop in my mind. The intense pain was delayed a few moments as if to allow the full gravity of the blessing I had just had placed upon me, to really sink in. "How do you feel? Are you okay?" Raine and Mckayla asked, to which I replied that I had never felt better. I was alive! So when my daughter asked if she could go into the water again, I glanced down at a nice spot on the sand that looked perfect for me to relax on and replied, "Sure!" At this point, we began seeing the signs of my concussion.

The pressure immediately began to build in my neck and at the base of my skull. I was also having difficulty swallowing and speaking, feeling constriction in my throat and pain to my trachea. The initial jolt of searing pain that shot down my spine in the water was now resolving into a radiating burn. We slowly and very cautiously ambled to the parking lot after Raine convinced me that I was in no shape to drive, and she took me to the nearest emergency room.

With advice from my wonderful husband who had received training in emergency field medicine in the Marine Corps, we placed a tennis shoe on both sides of my neck with the opening facing forward and wrapped my head with a towel, thereby not only securing my head and neck for the ride but also bringing some comfort with the slight pressure. The pain was increasing.

The concussion became more apparent on the drive to the ER. I noticed subtle vision changes, such as a slight narrowing of my range of vision and a cloudiness. I also began having trouble coming up with words as if I had a stroke. The words purse, phone, and wallet completely alluded me as I attempted to ask my daughter to collect what I needed from the car. I was reduced to pantomiming phone and requesting "the thing that all the things go into." While in the ER, I seemed to lose all concept of time (conveniently); the four and a half hours we spent there seemed to fly by.

After fentanyl for the pain, a head CT, a CT angiogram to check the integrity of the carotid arteries in my neck, and tons of blood work, the doctor came back to deliver the verdict in a solemn voice; there was no evidence of spinal cord damage or brain swelling, but I had fractured the C1 vertebra. As he was speaking, a smile began creeping onto my face. I then asked him, "Are you saying I broke my neck?" In a calm, serious voice, he responded yes, to which I burst out into hysterical laughter! Of course I did. Leave it to me, it's always got to be something, and this time I stepped it up a notch!

The doctor stared at me a moment, glanced at Dustin, and then responded, "I've never gotten that reaction before." A phone consultation with the neurosurgeon in Oahu resulted in a discharge. By the grace of God, I did not yet need surgery. I would need to wear a super spiffy neck brace for five weeks and return for a repeat CT. The craziest part of all? I would only need to take a week off work! I had already taken a week's vacation for my friend's visit, so I would only need to use a couple of sick days, thereby leaving my sick leave stash barely touched for my pancreas transplant (more on that another time).

Three nights later, I had crashed on the couch; the only way I could sleep was sitting straight up, so the couch was the most comfortable despite waking up every couple of hours from the pain, when I woke up to the most intense nausea. I stumbled to the bathroom where I writhed on the floor drenched in sweat, hoping to expel whatever poison was wreaking havoc on my system. The discharge instructions I received from the ER explicitly said I should return if I experienced any nausea and vomiting, so Dustin took me back. More blood tests, IV fluids, and some Zofran later, I was feeling better, other than the omnipresent neck and back pain and headache. My nausea and vomiting were aftereffects of the concussion. Thank goodness. So we would not need to panic if it happened again.

Day four, I woke up after my pain medication would have already worn off, *not* feeling the need to rush to the medicine cabinet. This was the day my pain was improving. Sweet.

I am one lucky momma, in so many ways. The outpouring of love and support was once again overwhelming. Our church family organized a meal train for two weeks, taking turns to feed our family of four, despite my insistence that I was healing and heading back to work. Now I needed to do my part and relax so I could heal. That was the most challenging part, being still—no exercising, no cleaning, cooking, and playing with my kids; even cuddling was a challenge! But after all everyone had done for me, the *least* I could do was the *most* I could do. I know in my heart God heard the prayers, and I was healed.

Odd Presentations

For my son's tenth birthday, we had a get together at the house with over twenty people. Although I had been following a mostly ketogenic diet, I allowed myself to enjoy a couple hot dogs—no buns—and then a couple more, then a slice of cake, and another. Over the next two days, I slipped big time, enjoying two or three slices of the four-layer Minecraft cake throughout the day and most of the leftover pack of BBQ'd hot dogs from the party. The day after the party, I noticed my left thumb was sore and swollen. Two days after the party, and after we had finally polished off the leftovers, I noticed my ankles were stinging, and my feet were swollen. Three days after that, I took the kids swimming, and I felt more short of breath while doing laps, not to mention extremely sore in the neck and shoulders with a general bodily weakness. The soreness could be explained by the workout I had done the day before; I was still building my strength up after breaking my neck six months prior. When rinsing off after swimming, I noticed my palms were yellow, and my hair was coming off in my hands. My reflection in the car's rearview mirror showed an amber tint.

Although I was eating way too much sugar for these three days, I was taking insulin to compensate, so my blood sugar levels were not too out of range. But the signs were clear—I was still doing myself harm. My daughter nervously asked if we should go to the hospital. The poor girl has already seen and helped her train wreck of a mom through so many health issues, but I refused. My out-of-pocket health insurance did not kick in for another two weeks since I was still in between jobs, and besides, I knew what the problems were and what I could do to get back on track.

The jaundice was my liver acting up. Although I hadn't drunk alcohol in over a year, I knew the drastic changes of blood sugar caused by my high sugar intake and insulin corrections would stress out my body. I could assume the hair loss could also be due to my blood sugars. The swelling to my hands and feet was probably due to my recent high salt intake. The swelling to my thumb, maybe a touch of gout? If that were the case, I could handle that too. After all those hot dogs, it would be no surprise that the uric acid would accumulate to form crystals in the joint causing pain and swelling. I should be able to cut out the foods high in uric acid to relieve the symptoms in my thumb. Any damage to my liver, I would not be able to repair, sadly, but I certainly knew how to make my liver happier with diet. Decreasing my caffeine and salt intake and increasing my intake of vegetables—luckily I have a garden full of kale and spinach—gentle exercise and stretching for my fatigued body, making sure I drank plenty of water, and cutting the sugar back out, I'd be good as gold or at least a less tarnished silver. And hey, maybe it was time for a haircut and a great wig!

On day four, Dustin spiked a fever of 103 and became sick as well. Although his symptoms were less broad, they were more intense. I never developed a fever, but after three more days, the swelling to my thumb and feet, yellowing of my skin, and hair loss seemed to resolve themselves. The sudden weight gain I had also experienced, approximately five pounds, also resolved. As the headaches and vomiting ceased as well, I realized my symptoms may have not been due to my decisions at our party, but rather a reaction to the virus my body was working to fight off. We all tested for COVID to be safe. Negative.

Now that Dustin and I have recovered from the bug, whatever it was, my body seems to have returned to baseline. My color and weight are back to normal, and my hair loss seems to have slowed back down; Dustin did not experience any of these odd symptoms. Interesting.

Chapter 6

Loss and Finding Strength in God

Peace I leave with you, My peace I give to you;
not as the world gives do I give to you. Let not
your heart be troubled, neither let it be afraid.
                                    —John 15:27 (NKJV)

Problematic Genes and Grudge Avoidance

In 2012, while living in Oklahoma, working part time as a home health nurse and caring for the kiddos, one being under the age of one, I got a call that my biological father Jim was in the hospital and very ill. At the time, Dustin, in the Marine Corps, was in California for work; so if I were going to travel to Oregon to visit my father during what was probably his final days, the kids would be coming with me.

My father and I were never close. He was my father by blood, but after having met him only a couple of times (at least while I was old enough to remember) and getting over the pointless resentment at his absence, I began to write him letters, often very brief—otherwise, they'd never get sent—but always including tidbits, initially about the goings on in my life and then later about his grandchildren. My mother and I left him when I was only one, him not being in the right place mentally to be a father yet again with my mom, eighteen years his junior.

When my sweetheart of six years and I tied the knot, I invited Jim to the wedding. I wanted him to be in my life. My mom asked how I would feel about him walking me halfway down the aisle and Larry, my stepdad, could walk me down the second half. This idea seemed absurd to me; Jim wasn't present for half my life, so he did not get to walk me down the aisle. Larry was my dad, the only dad I had ever known. Jim did not come to the wedding, and I was angry with him.

A year after our wedding, I sat at our tiny kitchen table in our tiny apartment in Point Loma, California, and wrote the first of many letters to him, making an attempt to keep up a relationship. I cannot remember if he responded to my letters, maybe once or twice in the next five or so years, but I kept writing. I hoped he was getting my letters, and that was enough for me. I was no longer angry. What good would that do? It would only cause pain, and I'm not a big fan of holding grudges. So when I got the call that he was in the hospital, I knew I needed to try to see him one last time.

I have it driven in my brain the idea that things in life happen for a reason. If they do not happen the way you want them to, it is to make you stronger, open other doors, and is all part of God's grander plan. And in my grief, I kept that in mind as plane flight after flight did not meet our budget. I would not be able to pack up the kids and fly from Oklahoma to Oregon.

I revved up the courage to call my father despite my obnoxious telephobia; at the time the anticipation of initiating a telephone call would leave me frozen with anxiety. This was going to be a tough call even under the best of circumstances. The nice staff at the hospital informed me that he had not been eating, and his body was shutting down due to the massive amounts of alcohol it had been living on for years. His organs were failing, and he was suffering delirium due to detox from not having alcohol while in the hospital. When I called his room, the nurse answered and handed the phone to him. I explained to him who I was—we had not spoken for over ten years—and his response was unintelligible. I tried to keep talking even though I was so nervous, possibly due to the fact that I was basically saying goodbye to this stranger that was my father. He kept mumbling incoherently on the line. I managed to choke out that I would try to call tomorrow and I loved him, a slightly awkward statement since in effort to be truthful I had been unable to write the words "I love you" in the past, much less say it. And the last words he uttered before we hung up were, "I love you too." The only words I understood, from the man who helped give me life thirty years prior, from this intelligent, artistic, mountain of a man, were the words I needed to hear more than anything else in that moment.

I was unable to make it to the small service, if it could even be called that. It was a simple burial. But the idea that all things happen for a reason brought me great peace. My older half sisters and half brother who I had met just months before via social media were there to sort through his very meager belongings and prepare his small home for the sale that would barely cover the cost of his debts. In his home, they found, displayed in plain sight, pictures of his grandkids, our little man and baby girl. He got my letters, and he knew about his granddaughter and grandson. He knew I wanted him to be part of our lives, but for reasons all his own, he could not write back.

Hearing those final words was an incredible gift, one that I will never forget. And I will never feel anger toward him. How could I? He gave me his giant chin! I have my mother's broad shoulders, fine hair, love for art, and reading. Someday I will get back in touch with my half siblings on his side and learn more about him, but that will have to wait.

So with all that said, the day after he died, I stopped drinking. I stopped drinking for two years and felt fabulous. Alcoholism was in my blood, and I would not go down the same path he followed. His manner of passing was an incredible motivator. My seizures are also a powerful motivator, but apparently not as long-lasting.

The Very Unexpected Loss of My Dad

"Wow. Wow," that was all I could say, with my hand covering my mouth, my feet stepping forward of their own volition into the large private room. "Wow." Lining the walls sat chairs, small tables with tissue boxes placed strategically, the center of the room a great empty space, pleasantly lit and tactfully decorated. Turning to my left, I saw laying on a gurney against the far wall of the room my dad Larry.

I have never been at a loss for words, but there were no words to describe the absolute, what? Shock? No, not shock. I thought I knew what to expect, although obviously I didn't. I don't think I expected him to look so much like *him*, so normal, as if he was simply taking a nap. I put my hand over his, feeling how cold and hard it was. I stared at his unsleeping face, knowing the truth but still waiting for him to blink or take a breath. His hair was brushed away from his face revealing the tan line from his hair that would fall on his forehead on the rare occasion he wasn't wearing one of his many hats. After staring at him for what may have been seconds or minutes, I needed to see. Afraid to lift the blanket, I called Dustin back to me. I think he was trying to give me space or simply needed a moment for himself. Under the plain white sheet draped over him, my dad was wearing a hospital gown. I reached to take his hand and bring it out and then the other hand to reveal what I needed to know without a doubt. Bandages covered both wrists. Abrasions covered his forearms. He had done it—he had taken his life. This left no doubt.

Larry was really my stepdad, but he was the only dad I knew. Jim, my biological father, and I never had much of a relationship. From the age of seven, Larry was Dad. He was the one to walk me down the aisle, so nervous I had to pull him back from running down the aisle with me on his arm. He was the one to cut my first child's umbilical cord when Dustin was on a ship in the middle of the ocean. He was Dad.

I always had a feeling he would die young. His father died at a young age, riddled with poor health, the stress of running his own company, and an affinity for too much alcohol. My dad inherited his high blood pressure and also struggled with drinking. The last we had talked, he told me he was doing well, drinking only occasionally after having quit for months. So when I got the call, alone in my living room with Dusty on the way home from picking up the kids, I was not immediately shocked when his wife's sister called me and told me, "It's about your dad." The knockout punch (I dropped to the floor) was hearing he had taken his own life. There was mention of it possibly being an accident. The police found no weapon except for a stick with blood on it. He had been drunk at the park. There was evidence he had fallen (abrasions on his arms) and may have landed on a stick. Slim chance, obviously. I'm sure the information was intended to soften the blow. Seeing that both of his wrists were covered at the mortuary was all the proof I needed.

My dad was always such a jovial man, eager to help his neighbors, always looking out for everyone else. When he had had too much to drink, he was an emotional man, prone to angry outbursts or emotional tears, but never, ever abusive. What I, along with most everyone else aside from one or two others, didn't know was that he was incredibly depressed. He was drinking so much he would be unable to get off the floor some days (yes, days). I don't know why. He never told me. Then again, I never told him about my emotional turmoil either.

It would be easy for me to dwell in *what if*, *if only*, and *I should have* myself to insanity. I still, four years later, slip up and catch myself thinking about what if I had never moved across the Pacific? What if I didn't take his only grandchildren away from him? What if I had made more of an effort to visit in the three years since we had moved to Hawaii or tried harder to keep him in touch with the kids? But I know that does no good. Doubt, regret, it's useless. He was in pain, incredible emotional pain. He decided to spare me from that knowledge, and of course I wish he hadn't, but I understand. For years, I felt the need to do the same, put on a brave front and tough it out. I do not know why he did it, and I do not need to know. I do not need to question God, how He could allow my dad to feel such pain and how He could take him away so soon. Not needing all the answers brings me peace.

No funerals in our family. No, we have celebrations of life. And what a celebration it was. Maybe fifty people came to show their love and support and to share good food and great stories about the man my dad was. In the beginning, I got up and spoke the words I had rehearsed in my head while walking for miles every morning to clear my head and organize my thoughts. I let everyone know I refused to be mad or question why and that he would want a party, along with another fifteen minutes of hopefully uplifting rather than depressing talk. I walked around grinning like an idiot, relishing in all the beautiful people who came, meeting some of my dad's oldest friends, and enjoying everyone's company. He had a great many friends, many of which I consider my family.

Unlike when my father's body shut down from too many years of alcohol dependency, driving me to quit drinking for two years, all I wanted to do when Dad died was to have a drink. I could not eat; for two weeks, I would manage a bite or two, but I mostly drank juice when I needed to for my blood sugar. I was never drunk during that time, but I just wanted to drink to dull the edges a little. It didn't work, however. Nothing made it less painful. Being around all those people, making the mortuary arrangements, and planning for the party kept me busy. I walked for quiet, swam for exercise, and talked for distraction.

It wasn't until I got home that it hit—the crushing absence of my dad. Returning to church, our dear friends prayed for me as I felt the hot tears spring forth in front of everyone, but felt loved. I felt so tired, so sad. I talked and talked and talked, to family, friends, and Dustin. I started to wonder if this was going on too long, if this was how I was supposed to feel. About the time Dustin suggested I talk with someone who was not connected with the situation for a fresh perspective, I felt the storm in my heart calming. I started to slip back into the home routine.

After seeing my dad laying on the gurney, something shifted inside me. It became real, true, that he was really gone. That night, I spoke to him as I fell asleep. I still speak to him, usually just to tell him I love him, I miss him, and I look forward to seeing him again. The pain doesn't ever go away; it just becomes less consuming, less sharp. I miss him so much more somehow, knowing he's not back in San Diego sitting in his patio chair reading the paper while watching the baseball game with his awesome wife Rose. I know I'll see him again, and I can't wait for one of those awesome hugs when he envelopes me in his arms, making me feel small and safe again like a little girl.

Light in the Dark

As each one has received a gift, minister
it to one another, as good stewards
of the manifold grace of God.
  —1 Peter 4:10 (NKJV)

It's difficult to imagine anything good coming from suicide, much less from the suicide of your own dad.

During my time as a hospice nurse, I saw death all the time. I have lost count of how many I have pronounced. I had begun to worry that I was becoming numb to death, cold, as if it didn't provoke any emotional response in me anymore. There I was, with family members at the saddest moments in their lives having lost their loved ones, and I was concerned my condolences were coming across as fake and shallow. Of course my sympathy was sincere for the surviving family, but it just felt forced to me. I struggled with what to say, sometimes opting to say nothing at all assuming my words would be meaningless to someone else.

It took my dad's passing to understand how to better empathize with people who had suffered loss. I now know those words, however few, offered from someone else intending to give sympathy and support, *do* matter. They come through as meaningful. I feel that I can now better relate to surviving friends and family, having lost someone close to me myself.

Upon returning to work after taking a week off after his passing, I learned one of the patients I visit frequently was having suicidal thoughts. This is not uncommon working in hospice as sometimes people are in pain or feel as if they are a burden to their families. Knowing him fairly well and knowing that he had a daughter and granddaughter, we sat down on one of our visits, and I shared with him my experience of my own dad committing suicide. I was able to offer him a different and very honest perspective about the effect it had on me. I explained that no one would feel better off without him and that caring for family members does not feel like a burden, but rather something we do because we love them. I cannot be sure, but I like to think sharing with him may have helped calm his fears.

I signed up for a charity benefit Out of the Darkness in support of suicide awareness and survivors. The emotional high I got after receiving the first donation toward the cause left me in tears. The second donation had me dancing to music in my kitchen resulting in silly smiles and looks of "What the heck is wrong with Mom?"—one of my favorite looks from the kids.

I had that feeling because those funds may help someone, maybe even just one single soul, struggling and in pain. So this is something positive coming from the loss of my dad. Although I was not able to help him and I miss him more than words can express, he has taught me a lesson. He has given me a gift, a way to relate to someone suffering a loss or struggling with the desire to end their own lives.

I actually raised more funds than anyone else participating. The walk was simple, up and down the main street of a small town in Hawaii, simple, but powerful. People honked horns, waved, and smiled at us. All the people I walked with had suffered their own loss or survived their own suicide attempts. After the walk, we all filled tiny jars with colored sand, each color representing a different manner of suffering. Once you had filled your own tiny jar, you took your own colored sand and filled others' jars so that no one had an empty jar. We wore beaded necklaces with these same colors. I was stunned to note the people who wore multiple colors for each person, their own child lost, a friend, a parent, and/or uncle. So much loss reflected in these little beads, yet so many smiles, hugs, and laughter from these brave people around me. Humanity never ceases to amaze me. Just beautiful.

Chapter 7

Little Miracles

But He said, the things which are impossible
with man are possible with God.
— Luke 18:27 (NKJV)

Occasionally I wonder if people think we're in a cult. God has such a huge part in our lives. We go to church on Sundays and Wednesdays. We socialize with our church family. Our kids have sleepovers with friends from church. Sometimes I feel like it's all I talk about. But even before we had found this church we love, and before my faith was at the forefront of all I do, I was grateful. I thank God constantly. I see butterflies flit past me and smile. I feel a glorious breeze on a warm day and spread my arms and tilt my head to the sun like a lunatic. I am so overcome with gratitude that I cannot contain it, and it often comes pouring out of me, filling me with a childlike abandon. And although when I had set out to write this little book, I really did not plan to go into my faith much more than the significant bits. I realize it's all significant; all the ways God has intervened in my life, it would be an injustice not to share it.

Believing in Jesus has not come easy for me as I have mentioned before. And once I felt secure in my belief in a higher power, I still felt like I didn't deserve to ask for God's grace. I would pray for others on a grand scale, careful to avoid praying for myself. Who was I to ask for help with work or my own health? When I came to believe in Jesus, I slowly started to pray more. It was when I came to understand that Jesus died for me and for my children, when I came to imagine meeting Him some day, giving Him a hug and saying thank you, that I realized I can ask God for what I need. I can talk to God like a father. I am His child; we all are.

So I pray. My husband and I pray. We were in a very challenging situation at one point in our lives where things just seem to be working out. We were living on our family's land trying to build a home, essentially camping. Our surroundings were beautiful and secluded. We did not have to pay rent, and we were close to our family. The kids could play freely. It was beautiful. But for one reason after another, we could not be productive. For two years, we met one obstacle after another while trying to build our home. This was the time I suffered my heart scare.

A few months before the stress and hopelessness of the situation hit its apex, we discovered our church Hamakua Baptist in Laupahoehoe. We began to pray more fervently. I began to be more specific in asking for guidance, strength, and some sort of resolution of our situation. Unfortunately the stress between ourselves and our family who had kindly let us reside on their land exploded into an argument that could not be easily repaired, and we decided to walk out on our plans to build. This decision was a painful one. We had put so much time and money into our plan, as did our family who had helped us, that it was one of the hardest things we had to do. And it caused a rift that took years to repair.

So here is where we get to the miracles. Let me preclude this part of the story with a bit about what it's like to live in Hawaii. It's expensive, really expensive. There are good reasons why so many people move to Hawaii to live their dream life, only to pack up and return to the mainland a year later. Housing does not come easily. It is difficult to afford something comfortable with a family and dogs. On one particular night, when the tension of working and living with family came to a climax, we gave our not-so-subtle notice of intent to vacate, and we began searching for a place to live, knowing we would need to have low expectations. We knew we would be lucky to find a one-or two-bedroom on a quarter acre an hour from work. More prayers and two days later, a small house popped up on Craigslist with a huge gated yard, totally within our budget. It's tiny but adorable, with a huge enclosed lanai (the Hawaiian word for patio) that would work well as a room for the kids. This may not sound ideal, but after living two years outdoors, getting rained on and stepping on slugs, it was a haven. The fact it was affordable, clean, and in a beautiful area, plus it popped up when we needed it most when there were no other options, miracle number one.

Remember all those lovely car problems? Yeah, those still existed. My Jeep Grand Cherokee was becoming a money pit. It left me stranded, refusing to start after shopping or simply shut off while driving. Luckily my handsome jack-of-all-trades husband was able to fix many issues, undoubtedly saving us thousands of dollars, but when the engine needed to be replaced, we knew we were in trouble. The new engine would cost us thousands, and we certainly could not sell the car for near what we owed on it. We were stumped. More prayers.

One weekend, I was on call for work, and returning from a home visit alone in my car, I smelled smoke. My mind might have turned to a possible backyard burn where people burn yard trimmings, paperwork, etc.; but given I was driving a ticking time bomb (yeah, I didn't exactly feel safe in this car), I knew it had to be the jeep and planned to inform the Dustin as soon as possible. After I parked next to the house (our sweet little cottage with the luxury of walls), my nine-year-old daughter pointed to the ground and said, "Something's burning." Sure enough there were embers in a couple of spots where I had just driven. My husband who had been working in the yard walked over, and we saw smoke coming from under my car. He decided to move it so that it didn't catch the house on fire. When he started the engine, a fire spontaneously ignited underneath, and flames rose up on all sides up as high as the windows. He jumped out and grabbed the hose quickly dousing the flames. He and I pushed the car into the yard away from the house and called the fire department, which arrived minutes later. We were miles away from any fire department, but our next-door neighbor was conveniently a volunteer firefighter and came right over. The flames did not reignite. My husband was not injured. Nether our children nor myself was anywhere near the car when it caught fire. We could have been in it! Miracle number two. Apparently a stick had gotten lodged up under the car, puncturing the fuel line somehow, and in such a way there was enough friction to burn it. From what I'm told, for this to happen is near impossible.

I was never going to drive this death trap ever again if I could help it.

The insurance representative came out to inspect it, a kind man with a story of his own, which I was more than happy to hear. I expressed my fear of ever driving it due to the possibility of combustion, which was not exaggerated, and he promised he would do all he could to declare it totaled. Have I mentioned how terrified I was of the hunk of metal? The problem was, if it was totaled, there was no way the insurance company would reimburse us for the total amount we owed. So not only would we need to go car shopping (and let me tell you we were not rolling in the dough; remember crazy expensive Hawaii?), but also we would need to pay off the remainder of our car loan before we could get another or take out another loan to pay off that one. I don't know how all that works best; I'm not big on money stuff. More prayers. After a stressful couple of days and a jazzy little rental car, I got the call from my husband; not only was the insurance going to reimburse us for enough to pay off the remainder of the loan, but also we would receive a little extra. Above blue book value! I burst out into sobbing tears, thanking God. Miracle number three.

This next little miracle is a very sad one, in that it cost us our family dog, Muttlee, so named because he was a scrawny little runt of a puppy when my husband found him on the road about to be hit by a car. His back legs hardly worked, and he was skin and bones. I nicknamed him Skelator in hopes of not getting attached. We had just gotten a puppy, and I was stressed out as it was. My brother-in-law called him Bruce Lee jokingly, then Mutt Lee, and eventually the name Muttlee stuck. I came to love this darn dog, but he was troubled from the beginning. He was a hunter by nature; we think he may have been born from a hunting dog that had gotten loose and had puppies in the forest. He would voraciously steal the other dogs' food, which we attributed to him having been starved for who knows how long. He began growling at the other dogs for their food, but when yelled at, he'd back off.

Our old girl Penny, a boxer / pit bull mix, died at about fourteen, so it was down to our two male pups. I should add, our pit bull mix never hurt a soul; she was always gentle and loving with the kids. A few years after we brought him home, Muttlee was growling at our other dog for his food. I yelled at him and swatted him on the back leg, not hard enough to hurt. He looked right at me and snarled. I, being the alpha over this mutt, grabbed him by the scuff and said firmly, "No!" He then lunged at me, hooking one fang under my chin and another through my lip. Somehow I got him off—that part is all a blank—and held him at arm's length with one hand, covering my mouth with the other, which at this point was dripping blood through my fingers. Dustin heard the commotion and came outside, grabbing Muttlee so that I could go try to stop the bleeding. My daughter came running to me asking what happened and saw me sobbing while washing my face with soap and water. I promised her through the tears that it did not hurt that bad. I was crying because I knew we could no longer keep Muttlee. And that was the truth. As soon as the adrenaline in my system slowed enough for me to think clearly, I became devastated that he was dangerous and could no longer live with us. My heart hurt. My lip was split, so I drove myself to the ER, and Dustin stayed with the kids since I adamantly refused that he drive me. I might be a bit stubborn at times.

All I could think as I drove to the ER was, *Thank you, God. Thank you, God. Thank you, God.* Our son had fed our three dogs for years; it has been his chore since he was four. When fifty-pound Muttlee would start trying to steal the other dogs' food, our son would nudge him away and tell him, "No, Muttlee!" It could have been him. That dog could have bitten our son, and he could have killed him, but Muttlee attacked me. And all I have to show for it is a small scar on my lip. I'm shaking as I write this as if a touch of the adrenaline is rushing through my system once again. Thank you, God.

My broken neck? Yet another miracle. I am blessed to be walking today.

These events may not seem big enough to call a miracle in your eyes, reader. But to our family, we feel like God reached down and gave us a hand. This makes me a little sad to report and a little selfish honestly. I know there is such suffering all over the world, and people with much greater needs than ours. But I feel it's so important to share, to spread the knowledge of the power of prayer and God's love.

Faith and Family

Wait on the Lord; be of good courage, and He shall
strengthen your heart; wait I say, on the Lord!
—Psalm 27:14 (NKJV)

I most often pray for guidance. Gavin always seemed to have a talent for trouble at school. He is very bright but seemed to have difficulty understanding personal boundaries and socializing. At one point, we were considering having him tested for ADHD so that we could identify ways we might be able to help him. We are very hands on with the kids' education, involved with the school however possible, e-mailing the teachers, administration, and the counselor; so we were working constantly on helping our son to control these issues. We felt that too much time was being wasted in school at addressing these concerns, and he was not getting the education he deserved. I began supplementing his education at home and discovered he was a whiz at mental math, able to multiply in first grade and was reading with ease. At the same time, my daughter who has always been at the head of her class admitted to me that she was struggling with math concepts and was not getting the assistance she needed at school. Among all this mess, there were public social issues being discussed that we felt had no place in school. Certain things should be taught at home, not at school. School is for academics. The public school system was becoming a place we did not want to be teaching our children. This feeling made me sick to my stomach. Something had to change.

Dustin and I had long discussed homeschooling the kids, but he and I both worked full time and didn't think we could swing the loss of income should one of us go part time. Around this time, I began talking with a friend at church about fostering children. It seemed like a dream; no way could we make that happen! As I learned more about all the children who were terribly abused, in awful ways I never thought humanly possible right here on our island, a seed of compassion seemed to plant itself in my mind. Our home is a relatively peaceful one. Oh sure, it's chaotic at times, disorganized, and messy; and sure, we raise voices now and then, but there is a lot of love too. I thank God every day for the man I met over twenty years ago and the healthy, happy children we brought into this world. So if there are children suffering out there, and there was something we could do to help them, even if we simply offered them shelter while their parents healed, why shouldn't we? So this seed of compassion began to blossom into something I couldn't ignore.

I prayed. *Please God, guide me. Please help me to make the right decision for our family. Please help me to see our path.* I prayed these words over and over again. Then one day, a statement comes to my mind while sitting in church. It was in my own voice, not just a fleeting thought or idea, but a definitive statement. I thought, *I will talk to my boss about going part time. I will homeschool the kids. We will be foster parents.* For the rest of the day, I was elated, excited, and motivated. I felt I had been given a gift, a message, and a plan. I talked to my husband, who thankfully does not think I'm completely crazy, and asked what he thought. We decided to try to come up with a definitive plan.

The next day, the elation evaporated, replaced with fear. Was this the right plan? Was that really God answering my prayers asking for guidance? Will we be able to afford it? Can I really handle teaching the kids? I decided quickly that yes, this was the path, and I would work on it starting now.

The first step was talking to my boss to work out how I could go part time and still retain my benefits. Turns out the answer was flat out no. There were no part-time positions. The governing board would not approve it due to the cost of insuring part-time employees and the fact that another nurse would need to be hired to see patients during the day so that I could only be on call. Well, of course it wouldn't be that easy. One thing I've learned is that things that do not come easily are somehow more valuable. The harder you work for something, the more you appreciate and value it. I was temporarily discouraged but pursued this course with a passion. I lost sleep over it. I e-mailed the director and the accountant. I believe my persistence made it very clear how important this was to our family. I had worked four years with the company at this point, and possibly I hinted that I may have to resign should I not be able to go down to part time. After almost two months, I got the call that all was approved. I could go part time, being on call on weekends and nights. After tears and thank-yous, I hung up with a plan to homeschool the kids after the end of the current school year. Persistence and prayer are a powerful combination.

Adventures in Fostering

*Give justice to the weak and the fatherless;
maintain the right of the afflicted and the
destitute. Rescue the weak and the needy;
deliver them from the hand of the wicked.*
—Psalm 82:3–4 (NKJV)

Life never really goes according to *our* plans, does it? But life does go according to *His* plans! We have this tiny, narrow view of what we think our life should be, such grand plans in our eyes, but what are they to God? Minuscule. God has the bigger picture, the full movie all planned out, with each actor's parts set in stone leaving room for free will's improvisations.

I feel incredibly blessed to have had a couple of my prayers for guidance answered with a snippet of a plan, like it was obvious all along what I should do, go to part time, homeschool the kids, and become foster parents. That straightforward, that simple—well, it wasn't simple in the doing of course. We followed the queues and all went relatively smoothly for a year. Then things changed. I got sick, insurance issues, money issues, etc. Life, you know?

Through all this I have held firm in the knowledge that it's all part of God's plan. I am *not* in control. But I do have to work at it. I have no fantasies of having a perfect life placed at my feet because I deserve it or any such nonsense. In 2019, I prayed to God, *Please let me know if I'm on the right path. Please help me to follow you and do your will.*

A few nights later, I had the most glorious dream. I was following Jesus like so many of the masses just to hear Him speak as He walked across the grassy hillsides. I was dressed in a long dark gown as the women in those times, except there was something different about me, something that made me stand out from the crowd. I did not belong there. I was sick, a sinner. Not only did I see Jesus and speak with Him, but also He took me by the arm, I heard His gentle voice, and we walked together. I walked the pathway with Jesus. I can't recall what we talked about. I don't think that was the point.

When I walked in my daughter's room the next morning, I saw the furry black coat that I had been wearing in the dream, the coat I haven't seen in forever, laying on the floor of her room. It all came flooding back to me. I then felt rejuvenated. I was now even more motivated to keep going with the plan God had set for me. I was walking with God, He loves me, and that's what really matters.

My dear friend from church Emily Rogers is a foster mother and has three biological children of her own, five adopted and two foster children. She and her husband have opened their home and hearts to help foster children with disabilities as well. She inspired me with her gentle kindness and fearless faith in God. In fact, it was she who invited me to Hamakua Baptist Church for the first time, the same church family we have been a part of for over three years now, the same church that has changed our lives for the better. Emily never made me feel pressured to foster, but through her love for the foster children of Hawaii, I began to see the need for foster parents, also known as resource caregivers. I was astounded to learn of the mistreatment of children that occurs every day and not only out in the world but also on our very own island. I heard stories about children kept in cages, locked in rooms with no food, witnessing abuses to their loved ones, or suffering through physical, emotional, and sexual abuse themselves. I was so naive to the atrocities that humans are capable of where children are involved. Even foster parents could be abusive, mistreating the children placed in their care in order to collect money from the system. I felt an overwhelming calling to become involved.

My husband and I became certified to foster with plans to help children. Our kids were seven and eleven at the time.

Our first experience with fostering, not having children placed with us permanently, was a three-week respite, meaning the child would stay with us temporarily rather than the foster family. This does not require certification and can be done by anyone wishing to help. He was an adorable one-year-old, an absolute doll, but had trouble sleeping at night. Having him around and realizing how impossible it was to get things done with a one-year-old again crawling everywhere made me rethink my preference for a baby for our first-time fostering experience.

Around the time he went back to his foster family, I realized my health issues were worsening so I decided to use up my vacation and sick time from work to take a little time off. The very last night I was on call for work, I received a call from the Department of Human Services (DHS) looking to place two children, four-and five-year-old brothers. God's perfect timing strikes again. We took them in at midnight that night.

Their presentation was right out of the textbook, dirty and wearing torn clothes that did not fit properly. They were exhausted but sweet. They came right in and sat on the couch while I talked to the social worker. I got them tucked into bed (Dustin was asleep since he had to work the next day), and then I settled onto the couch for a restless night.

Early the next morning, I was awakened by the boys coming out into the living room with their small sacks they got at the hospital and wearing the same clothes from last night, worryingly stating (in very broken, difficult to understand English) that they needed to take the bus. The social worker informed me they had never been to school and never took the bus. This was just the first of many little mysteries these boys would have me scratching my head about.

The Honeymoon

The first week was rather peaceful. The boys were very well-behaved, quiet, and cooperative. All the kids got along great. I felt in control of the fact that for now, I had four kids! So many of the daily activities my family performs were a novelty to the boys. Daily showers with warm water and soap were a treat. They were excited to brush their teeth, and by the looks of their teeth, I'm not sure they ever had. We all went to the library, church, the park, and the grocery store together; and the boys were overwhelmed with joy at the newness of it all. Having their own bed and their own belongings was an astounding concept. This relatively calm, happy period was the honeymoon. The honeymoon was very temporary.

We quickly learned how little they had been taught how to do. They needed to be taught how to brush their teeth, how to use the toilet and wipe properly, and how to dress, bathe, and use eating utensils. They had been taught nothing of colors, shapes, numbers, or letters.

The little one (let's call him Nelson) began to wet the bed after the first few days, only occasionally at first and then every night. Waking him two hours after bed to use the bathroom seemed to help, but dry nights were still rare. The boys began fighting constantly, hitting, and cursing. We began to get an idea of what their homelife was like. I started with simple easy-to-remember rules such as no hitting or cursing. This evolved to no pushing, hitting, kicking, spitting, fake punching (because it always led to real punching), and no bad words; and these were punished consistently with loss of tech time and a "scolding" (not yelling) as the brothers called it. The concept of consistent consequences was very new to them; they were used to getting "licks" when they got into trouble, as evident by the bruising to big brother's face in the shape of a hand when they first came to us.

For a few weeks, we saw improvement. I began working on enrolling the boys in pre-K, and four-year-old Nelson being too young for pre-K, I worked on having him evaluated for special education pre-K. He undoubtedly had cognitive delays, difficulty following instruction, staring blankly when spoken to, etc. I later learned what I originally considered cognitive was emotional detachment. This process was painfully slow, and after two months, I was no closer to having him signed up for preschool.

Five-year-old—let's call him Jackson—was adjusting very well. He looked out for his little brother, and he was obviously genuinely trying to follow the rules and listen to *Auntie* and *Uncle* (as children often refer to adults in Hawaii). There was a maturity and independence about him far beyond his five years that I believe came from him needing to take care of his little brother since Mom and Dad could or would not. Again, textbook.

Little Nelson responded very well to one-on-one playtime when it was just the two of us. It was easy to get swept up in the chaos of life and all its demands. And sometimes it seemed like all he was interested in was seeking out trouble, but when I was able to sit with him and engage in any sort of play—Play-Doh, cars, Legos, etc.—his face would light up with the brightest smile, and I would see a peek at an innocent exuberance I rarely got to see otherwise.

Nelson began acting out more violently. He began screaming, purposely instigating fights with his brother and my son, and hitting more; and most concerning, he began being rough with the animals. He smacked the cat in the face with an open palm, squeezed the puppies until they squeaked, and threw rocks at the chickens. One morning, I woke up to a large pile of poop close to his bed and the next morning a puddle of what may have been urine. Our two dogs are inside dogs, so I was not 100 percent sure who was responsible, but I was certainly concerned. I maintained frequent contact with the boys' social worker.

We were working on having Nelson seen by a therapist; but the therapists, counselors, and psychiatrists seemed to be in high demand on our side of the island. Our goal was to help him however we could, but not at the detriment of our own family. We were afraid that if we requested he be placed elsewhere in what we may have thought was a healthier situation for him, he'd only get worse. So I tried to keep him close, having him stick with me through teeth brushing and showering, or he would get distracted and act out. For instance, one night while left alone to use the restroom, he sprayed an entire can of spray sunblock on the floor and in the toilet.

Slowly, disturbing facts emerged about how the boys lived. The most concerning aspect was how the boys would talk about events. They calmly and pleasantly stated facts at the dinner table that would astound us all with their atrocity, but to them, it was simply how normal people lived. We would do our best to keep a calm demeanor, while on the inside, we were outraged that children could be mistreated in such a way.

Neither of the boys had ever been to a dentist and would now need to have most of their teeth capped. Many of their teeth were broken, cracked, or simply decayed away to a stub. The pain in his teeth may have been part of the reason for Nelson's acting out. They were both excited to show off their silver crowns placed on many of their baby teeth after multiple trips to the dentist.

Little breakthroughs, laughter, hugs, and a wordless thank-you—it was all so humbling. These moments helped me to remember, when I was exhausted or questioning what we had gotten ourselves into, why we had decided to help these kiddos.

One day when I arrived to pick up Jackson from pre-K, he ran to me and gave me the biggest hug! I had been cautious (perhaps overly so) with physical contact, very careful to respect physical boundaries. I didn't give hugs without asking first. After the first month, I would place my hand on their backs, hold their hands when crossing the street, or tussle their hair. But for big brother to run to me for a hug? Super sweet and special!

Our goal was to continue to provide a safe, warm, clean home for our two new little friends. We would continue to teach them how to speak properly, manners, numbers, shapes and colors and how to treat one another without physical violence and kindness to animals. We would share with them the joy of simple things they had thus far been denied.

This was the first time the children had been removed from their home. The boys had weekly visits with Mom and Dad. On the way home from the first two visits, the boys would scream out to Mom and Dad in great tears and sobs and then again the night of the visit.

I don't believe they understood what was happening. They couldn't possibly grasp that the reason they were taken away from their family in the middle of the night was because their parents chose methamphetamine over and over again over their own five children.

After the first two months, the parents stopped coming to the visits. But on the last visit, the brothers' mother told me she was pregnant again.

I wish I could say the foster parenting classes didn't tell us how hard it would be to make the call that perhaps a placement wasn't the right fit, but now that I think on it, we did talk about it. There was just no preparation for how difficult it could be. So much of what we had seen during our first experience had been what we were told may happen, the acting out, shutting down emotionally, etc.

How Our Biological Children Were Affected

This experience was incredibly challenging for our children. Eleven-year-old Mckayla wasted no time in telling us how very miserable the boys made her. Although I pleaded with her to be understanding, empathetic, and patient, her distress was understandable. She went from having one annoying little brother to three, all of which *loved* to provoke her. She could be very helpful, especially when I was ill. She would play hide-and-seek, making them snacks. But once I started to feel better, her annoyance was overriding her concern for Mom, and she persisted in a state of aggravation while the boys were around. Luckily she was the only one in the house with her own room, so she had an escape.

Seven-year-old Gavin would sway between loving having two playmates to despising the air they breathed. He too was extremely helpful at times. When I was unable to get out of bed, he would make the boys waffles for breakfast or put on a movie for them all to watch. But he'd have full-on meltdowns every couple of days when something didn't go his way, the boys took his toys, or they simply would not give him any space. Looking back, I realize my worsening illness was an unfair extra burden on the kids.

However, I believe this experience helped them develop compassion, empathy, and appreciation for their own situation. One wonderful outcome of the fostering experience I had not anticipated is that it has brought our own biological children closer. They now have a powerful common experience to share, the struggles of having foster siblings. They would often play Minecraft or build Lego creations together in my daughter's room and seemed to enjoy their time together so much more.

Moving Forward

After a weekend of new concerns and feeling pushed to the brink of breaking, I realized our home, our routines, and our rules may not be the right situation for our youngest foster. He bit our son, and the day before, he and my son sprayed down the chicks with the hose set to jet, nearly killing two of them. What concerned me the most about the chickens was the lack of remorse or regret from Nelson. My son was devastated, near tears, when he learned what they did may result in the chicks' death. He prayed passionately for God's forgiveness and the chicks' recovery and kept repeating that he should not have listened to Nelson (who was three years younger than my son). The time came to talk to the social worker to ask about a therapeutic home or possibly a placement where he was the only child.

It astounds me that circumstances can affect you in such a profound way that you don't realize it till something is drastically changed. I didn't realize how significantly our stressful situation was affecting us emotionally.

Almost every day when my husband would come home, I would immediately vent to him on how much trouble the kids got into, how they had lost their desert and tech privileges, and how things were not getting better. Finally, he pointed out I always looked depressed, exhausted, and stressed. Although I was dealing with a mysterious health issue, I certainly did not consider myself unhappy. In fact, I was thrilled to be fulfilling God's calling by fostering and excited for us to be working toward buying our own home. But I came to realize that the stressful situation had affected us all more than I thought; I was losing myself, always yelling, refereeing arguments, and taking away privileges. Homeschool was near impossible. My daughter was stressed and angry, my son was having almost daily emotional meltdowns, and our older foster, although appearing comfortable, spent most of his time fighting with and trying to correct his younger brother in an attempt to keep him out of trouble.

Dustin and I talked and decided our home may not be the best environment for Nelson. He seemed to be having so much trouble adjusting. He was constantly provoking fights with all the other kids. He would not follow the house rules and continued to wet the bed almost nightly (a minor issue in the grander scheme of things). One of our most important rules was to never intentionally hurt others. He kept lashing out physically at the two other boys. We let the social worker know we thought it would be best for him to be placed elsewhere, with a family without small animals and perhaps no other children so that he could get the attention he seemed to need so desperately, and that sadly I was unable to provide while caring for three other children and dealing with health issues.

So I called the social worker to notify him the situation was not improving and was in fact causing harm to our family. A little over a week after the call, and three weeks after initially expressing concern, little brother was placed with another family. I took all the children together to the DHS office to drop him off so that he could go home with the family "that would like him to come stay with them." Neither of the boys seemed surprised. There were no sad goodbyes, just hugs and "see ya next week's." Big brother seemed understanding and calm.

This was so troubling because Dustin and I didn't wish to give up on him. We wanted to help him, not cause more damage; this was why we were fostering in the first place, fully knowing most children were troubled and traumatized by what has happened to them. I was concerned we could not help him, and that was devastating.

That night, the change was palpable. There was very little arguing and no yelling. The difference was like night and day with a very peaceful atmosphere.

The next day, we began to see a change in big brother. He began to act silly, always smiling. Within a couple of days, he was running up to both me and my husband for hugs and asking to be held. It seemed like he now felt permitted to be a kid without the added burden of caring for and constantly fighting with his younger brother. The boys' mother later informed me these two, out of a sibling group of five, fought the most.

Jackson and my son got along famously. They would play for hours outside, arguing now and then as children do, but it was never physical. My son no longer had meltdowns.

We were concerned that having his little brother placed in another home would only cause more emotional trauma. We hoped Nelson's next placement would be a better fit than our own home, so when we heard he was placed in a home with a litter of puppies and under the care of foster parents who ran a day care out of their home, we were very concerned. But we needed to care for our family, so we trusted all would work out for the best. We later learned he was doing well and no longer wetting the bed every night.

Perhaps he was no longer the youngest child in the home and no longer felt the need to lash out and seek trouble to get attention. Whatever the reason, he seemed happier when we saw him at the weekly visits.

I have to be honest, I still feel a tremendous amount of guilt for giving up on him. I tell myself that we had to do what was best for our family, but that voice in the back of my head mockingly asks, *Well, what did you expect, a perfect situation?* I know many foster children are working through significant emotional trauma, and I pray to God our decision works out for the best for both the boys. I do know in my heart it was a tough call that had to be made for the good of our family.

Jackson was a very cheerful, happy-go-lucky little dude, active, rambunctious, a very good listener, and never a complainer. But after three weeks of no visits with his mom and dad, we began to notice his very occasional quiet moments were becoming more frequent. He had started to seek attention for his sore spots that miraculously moved about his body and groaned now and then about not wanting to do one thing or another.

Almost six months after he had come to stay with us, he wet the bed, and then the same day, he had an accident while playing outside. He did not tell me when it had happened but was honest when I discovered it and asked him about it. I told him it was okay and that he was not in trouble, but I just needed to know so we could clean it up. I also encouraged him to stop playing and use the restroom as soon as he felt the urge. At his age, he knew these things of course, but I thought it important he knew he was not in trouble.

I became more aware and careful not to irritatedly respond, "What?" when he called my name for the hundredth time to ask me a question I had already answered twice that day. With the three kiddos running around, it was easy for the grumpiness to creep up on me when they were all demanding my attention, but I was trying my best to squash it down. Mckayla was also losing her patience, becoming very angry and jealous at the attention he received. It was so challenging for her to accept that while anyone was under our care, they would be considered part of our family, despite our insistence that no one would ever take her place.

I prayed we could make him feel loved and safe and that hopefully soon he would see his family again. It was heartbreaking to see his pain and sadness he didn't quite know how to express.

Saying Goodbye

The time came for us to say goodbye to our little foster buddy. DHS decided it would be in his best interest to be closer to his family and to attend school with his brothers. His brothers lived and attended school over an hour away from where we lived, so although we were willing to try to make it work, it seemed best for all that he moved in with his older brother.

The two brothers were in our care for the first two months, and they fought constantly. So when the idea of Jackson moving in with a brother came up, they organized a weekend sleepover to test the waters. Everyone got along great, and for the next three weeks, our little friend talked constantly, with joy about what he and his brother did, games they played, movies they watched, etc. I heard little of his potential new foster parents, but I hoped that was neither here nor there.

We broke the "exciting news" at the dinner table that he was going to get to move in with his brother so that they could go to school together and he would be closer to the rest of his family. The kids were all ecstatic, for different reasons of course. My daughter almost broke down in tears of relief, and our son seemed pleased he would get his room, toys, and privacy back.

Jackson did very well; he said goodbye, gave me a hug quickly, and left with his new foster family and his oldest brother. It was so brief, so easy, and very anticlimactic. I'm not sure what I was expecting.

My kiddos were cheerful after Jackson left. They would still play together, more so than they had before we had fosters. This experience had no doubt brought them closer. The house was a little quieter. I think the challenging part was not Jackson's absence—we knew this would be the case sooner or later—but the fact we were no longer in the loop. He became such an important little person in our lives, a puzzle piece that we adjusted our lives to fit in. His absence did not leave a hole, our family has knitted right back to how it was, but I was saddened some by the fact that I would no longer know how he was doing, how the court dates went, how he was doing in school, etc. It's an interesting feeling, being so concerned about a child and then to hand him over to someone else along with all the responsibilities and concerns, never to know about that child again.

Since our lives were about to get a bit more chaotic with starting a new school and career forty-five minutes from home, we decided to take a small hiatus from fostering, but we were definitely planning to open our hearts and homes to more little friends in the future.

We received a couple of calls from DHS asking to place children with us following Jackson's departure. Due to my long working hours, our situation became very specific. It would need to be a school-age child, able to stay in after school day care. After we turned down three placements, they stopped calling us. Although we are still licensed, we have not yet fostered again due to the confines of our lifestyle, but if the right situation presents itself, we are still open to help out.

Career Lessons

Trust in The Lord with all your heart
and lean not on your own understanding.
In all your ways submit to him, and
He will make your paths straight.
—Proverbs 3:5–6 (NKJV)

It's a terribly lonely feeling, the idea that you are on your own. The pressure of making a life-changing decision is a great burden, knowing that whatever you choose to do will affect not only you but also your entire family. I sadly watch Dustin toil under that pressure. He is an amazing father and a loving, supportive husband. He voluntarily takes on the responsibility of providing for us and protecting us. He affords us such a feeling of security I cannot imagine my life without his loving embrace. I believe he feels that burden and concern so much more than me, that if he makes the wrong decision, it might damage our future. Through our experiences, I have come to trust God all the more. I feel a sense of serenity that if our lives do not go according to our hopes and plans, it is because God had a different plan for us.

See, how he and I work, we seem to thrive in the chaos of life. When our situation becomes too calm and predictable, we add some new challenges. If we've become comfortable living in one spot for too many years, we decide it's time to move. When a career seems to be going well, maybe it needs to be changed. But we don't just move down the street. Oh no. We move to an island in the middle of the ocean!

Currently we are debating moving away from Hawaii in search of new opportunities. We want to take everything we've known for the past eight years, living on a tropical island, and turn it on its head. I want adventure, Dustin wants political stability, and the kids are excited for change.

The last two years have been challenging for us all. I have discovered something new living here in Hawaii, something I hadn't felt growing up as a white female in San Diego, the feeling of being an outsider. In Hawaii, people who move here are often referred to as *haoles* ('houlē), a person who is not native Hawaiian, more specifically white people. When we were discussing moving to Hawaii, my research and in speaking with people familiar with the culture, I learned this might be an issue with the children in school. For the first five years, I worked with an incredible association, North Hawaii Hospice, where I felt appreciated and loved. Occasionally a patient might treat me differently due to my not being from the island, requesting *no haole nurses.* I was usually able to win them over with a smile and an open heart, but generally people were warm, friendly, and welcoming.

The kids were three and six years old when we moved. They were able to make friends at school and suffered no treatment different than they would have on the mainland at first. We delved headfirst into discovering the culture and enjoyed learning about Hawaiian history, art, hula, etc. After a few years of this, we began to notice there was very little teaching of US history and the values we held so important. The public schools in general seemed to be teaching not nearly enough of what we considered core education such as math, science, and literature and seemed more focused on feelings rather than academics. At this time, we were also looking into becoming foster parents, so it worked out that we would homeschool, I would begin working on call at night for hospice, and we would foster.

During any transition in our life, any major decision, I pray for guidance. I pray for God to help us to make the right choice for our family so that we can pursue His plan for us. I do not feel the need to understand God's plan, but I would like to be in on it. I pray for a sign or some confirmation that we are on the right path. And I am learning to trust that little voice in my head, be it my conscience, or the guidance of God. I have discovered when I listen, things seem to work out. Trusting in God works; it really does.

As an extra incentive, Dustin's employer offered to pay for our children to go to private school when the time came for me to go back to work. When the lack of sleep caused a major health scare as a result of my taking call at night for two years, I found a new position working during the day in the biggest city on Hawaii Island, Hilo, at a community health center. We found a Catholic school just down the street. We were excited to discover a school that would include God in the curriculum while teaching Christian morals.

The new job offered a whole new set of stressors. My schedule was four eleven-hour days a week, so the kids attended the after-school program. Due to my day starting at 6:45 a.m., I would drop the kids off outside the school where they would wait in the dim light for the school to open at 7:00 a.m. This also meant we were leaving home at 5:50 a.m. One morning, there was a homeless man sleeping outside the front door to the school where I dropped them off. Mckayla nervously called me on her cell phone and left a message asking what to do as I did not see the man in the dim light when I dropped them off. I did not get the message until I was already at work, and when I repeatedly called her back, she didn't answer. I was terrified and turned right around to head back to the school. Moments later, she called my back to tell me one of the school staff let them in through a different door. *Thank God.* There was a public park in a grassy area behind the school. Although there was a large police station less than a block away from the park, it did not seem to deter the homeless from sleeping at the park nor drug dealers from making their deals at the public bathroom. This situation was not ideal.

The latest I could pick up the kids was 5:30 p.m., but I did not get off from work until 6:00 p.m. My mom lives twenty minutes from town, so she would pick them up and keep them in town to wait till I got off work. This became too challenging for her, and I began taking a fifteen-minute break at 5:15 p.m. to pick up the kids, and then they would wait in the car outside of my work until I got off work. Again, really not ideal, and my supervisor made it clear this could only be temporary.

The long days were challenging, not only for the kids but also for me. With the long drive into and back from town, we ended up being away from home for over thirteen hours, leaving little time for anything other than dinner and showers when we got home. But the job seemed challenging and new, and the kids were getting an undoubtedly fantastic education, so it seemed worth it.

Then the new-job honeymoon began to wear off. I was picking up the routine quickly, so I was assigned to a provider a month and a half into my three-month training period. The stress was absurd, and there was never enough time to give the patients the attention they deserved nor to complete all the miscellaneous tasks, something I discovered all the nurses and providers alike coped with on a daily basis. As the doctor (also new to the company and learning via crash course) and I learned together and developed a system to be as efficient as we could be, we were scheduled with more patients.

Having worked the last five years for North Hawaii Hospice, a nonprofit, I was new to the system of health care run as a moneymaker. From the higher-ups, the emphasis was placed on "providing quality care" to the maximum number of patients in order for the clinic to *maybe* make enough profit to stay up and running. This *quality care* is intended to occur over a twenty-minute visit—an absurd notion in my opinion anyhow. This is assuming the patient arrives twenty minutes early as instructed (which rarely happens) so that the nurse (that's me) can collect all the information, vital signs, conduct the surveys, collect history, etc. to prepare for the visit with the doctor so that their time can be as productive and helpful as possible.

Okay. So let's imagine that system works smoothly. Let's assume people arrive on time, the doctor is able to address their needs in twenty minutes, and we are able to see the recommended eighteen patients a day in order to make enough profit to make administration happy. This does not take into account the time it takes to accomplish the behind-the-scenes work, the prescriptions, the referrals, the provider's extensive research needed to diagnose patients, and the authorizations needed for MRIs, CTs, physical therapy, medical equipment, and pre-op documentation. It goes on and on.

The issue was there was never enough time. It didn't feel like quality care when you hardly had enough time to make eye contact with your patient, to listen to their pain, to nod sympathetically when they break down in tears from frustration when they feel like no one can help them, to give them a hug when they explain their fear of dying, or to blow up a glove balloon for their toddler so you can give the patient a moment to breathe. The patients were frustrated, angry, sad, or scared; and sometimes they took it out on me. And that's okay. I could take it. What I couldn't take was the feeling that I could not do a darned thing to help them. What brought me to tears when I got home was the feeling that despite all my lost sleep, weight gain, suffering health, and emotional turmoil, I was not making a difference.

During this time, I prayed so much. I asked God for a more positive attitude, to help me focus on the good, to not let the stress bring me down. I prayed for the strength to be good at my job and still have the energy to rock mommyhood and be the supportive loving wife my awesome husband deserved. I prayed for guidance, for God to place me where He needed me to be so that I am always doing His work. This job had not yet felt like where God wanted me to be. Fostering felt like God's work; this job did not.

The physician I worked with had also been stressed and frustrated for similar reasons. Finally, one day it came to me, my purpose. It was not up to me to heal these people. It was up to me to do my job thoroughly and efficiently so *the provider* could help heal these people. I would encourage and support while staying as upbeat as possible and continue to do my job the best I could. It seemed so simple, so obvious; yeah, duh, my purpose was to do my job. But it was more than that. I think I had been placed in that position not to move mountains, but rather to support the movers. I stuck it out and kept in mind that another door would open, and I would be ready for it, wiser and full of gratitude.

That next open door definitely did not present itself as I thought it would. My daughter, my little buddy, saw me struggling. As she came home stressed by all the work she had in school and the bullying she began to experience at her new school, I would be in tears due to all the stress at work. We would cry together. She said to me, "Mom, just quit!"

And I would explain, "No, I could not quit until I had another job lined up." I needed to be responsible not only to help my family but also to set a good example for my impressionable preteen.

Then There Was COVID

Before COVID, I seemed to catch every virus that was floating around. In the year I worked at the community health center, I had come to believe I definitely was immunocompromised as a type 1 diabetic, a fact I have been very reluctant to accept. I stayed active, exercised as often as I could, and ate well. So when I was quickly becoming short of breath on my runs, I attributed it to leftover congestion after my back-to-back flu and pneumonia (2020 was already off to a rough start). The breathlessness was not improving as it should have, but rather became unmanageable. I became winded while shopping. It became hard to take deep breaths. Finally, I developed a fever to accompany the chest pressure, constriction, and body ache.

At work, I was in close contact with more than twenty people a day to take vital signs. Any one of those people could have been infected, but more importantly, if I were infected, I could have given any one of those patients the virus. At the time, it seemed most people who caught the virus recovered with no ill effects, but if I were to infect our ninety-four-year-old cancer patient or the seventy-year-old with heart failure, there was a significant chance they would not survive. It was time to be tested.

In the very beginning of the COVID outbreak, testing sites were not yet established. So I first contacted the local ER, a very small office in a very small town closest to my home. When I asked on the phone if they conducted the test, there was obvious confusion, followed by a hold while the staff looked for protocol on a possible COVID-19 case person of interest (PUI). They did not have the testing capabilities, so they recommended I contact my primary care provider (PCP). My PCP suggested I contact the ER in one of the two larger towns closest to me. The large ER I contacted informed me there was drive-through testing available in the attached building, which was apparently closed but opened at 8:00 a.m. *Fantastic,* I thought, *we're not as behind on the testing curve as I feared!* When I spoke with the administrator who I was told would have more information, all they could tell me was that I needed a doctor's order. *Okay, I could work with that.* "Where would I send the order?" I asked. "Fax number? Could it be called in by phone?" Crickets. They had no idea. They instructed me to contact my provider who would know where to send the order. I was starting to feel like I was losing my mind. I called my provider, and they instructed me to go to the ER.

I drove to the ER and called from the parking lot, whereupon they instructed me to go to the drive-through. I explained I did not have a doctor's order, and they instructed me to come in. They directed me to the quarantine section, an area blocked off by a wall, and finally got me in. Once I was in, I was treated courteously, albeit something of an oddity. The doctor came in after the nurse had collected my vital signs. He was covered head to toe in a hazmat suit right out of a science fiction movie, with a large disposable helmet and a plastic viewing window. As he spoke, his voice was muffled but friendly, and he promptly tested for the flu, and another test was taken for the coronavirus should the flu come back negative. Large cotton-tipped applicators were pushed through each nostril and down to the back of my throat and left there for a full minute.

I was informed the flu test would be done by that afternoon, and if it came back negative, the second swab would be sent to Texas to test for COVID-19. Either way I would be notified through my provider of the flu test, and then the COVID test if done, in three days.

My employer was very understanding and, with the note from the ER, allowed me to stay home to await the test results.

After four days, still no results. I am a big fan of the squeaky wheel gets the grease method. I called my PCP multiple times, the ER, the lab, the hospital, and medical records. Not only were there no results for my flu test, but also there was no estimate on when my COVID test results would be available. And so I waited. Luckily my fever was down, and my chest pressure had stopped, but I was still becoming breathless with the slightest exertion.

Twelve days later and I was still waiting for the verdict.

I had exhausted my paid time off after the first week of waiting, and although my employer informed me if my symptoms had resolved, it was up to me whether or not I returned to work, I opted to stay home to await my results so that I did not endanger our patients or my coworkers. We were also informed that the nurses were prohibited from wearing masks unless working directly with someone suspected of having COVID-19.

After countless calls, I was still no closer to knowing whether or not I had COVID-19, so my family also stayed home. I volunteered to be laid off from my job. While health-care providers worldwide were struggling to hold on to their staff and hiring more nurses to meet the increased demand for care, my clinic was laying people off in order to save money. Sadly, I was all too willing to be free of an organization that places so little importance on people's well-being, of both the staff and the patients.

The facility where I was tested enacted a telephone line dedicated to providing test results. When I called again after two weeks, I was directed to leave a message. After almost three weeks, I received the results of my COVID test, negative. Although the stress of not knowing was frustrating, the side effects included more family time and an opportunity to leave a job I was miserable at. However, I did feel quite guilty about leaving amidst the COVID pandemic.

Another Door Opens

A soft answer turns away wrath, but a harsh word stirs up anger. The tongue of the wise uses knowledge rightly, but the mouth of fools pours forth foolishness.
—Proverbs 15:1–2 (NKJV)

After volunteering to be laid off from my position at the community health center, I obtained a new position working with a vascular surgeon in an outpatient clinic with a large medical center in Hawaii. Initially we were sharing a space with the general surgeons, but after about six months, we were given a separate space, a new office in which to grow. The surgeon, being the only vascular surgeon on the island, was extremely busy and in high demand, so administration hired a nurse practitioner (NP) and a medical assistant to help her. The NP was working for about two months before her assistant was hired, so I covered for both providers until she too became too busy and my supervisor needed to fill in to help cover. At this time, I didn't complain about the extra work, but I did make it clear that we needed to hire someone as soon as possible to assist the NP so that my struggling to cover both providers did not put them behind schedule.

I try to avoid gossiping, and when people start talking at work, I tend to keep my head down and get my work done. But in doing so, I isolate myself from the social group thereby getting left out from events outside of work. Unfortunately, this may also give people the impression that I'm a snob or unapproachable. This is far from the truth, but I suppose it cannot be helped.

Coming up on a year of employment, and feeling confident that I was doing my best while knowing areas I needed to improve on, it came as quite a shock when I started getting e-mails about the uneven distribution of workload and my changing attitude. After about a week of stomachaches, questioning my capabilities as a nurse, and wondering where I went so wrong, I met with the provider I worked with and my supervisor. It turns out these communications were being shared with not only myself but also our entire team. I felt awful. I felt hurt and betrayed by my team, which days prior felt so cohesive.

My coping method was prayer and talking things over with my family. They reinstilled the feeling that I was indeed a capable nurse, one who truly does care about her career and her patients. I prayed for patience, understanding, and peace of mind (my mind was caught up in a whirlwind of self-doubt and fear for the future of my career). At one point, I received a hurtful text message from my supervisor that left me stunned, so I prayed for her, asking God to help her through whatever she may be going through that may cause her to take out her pain or frustration unjustly on me.

When I returned to work after the weekend, I stayed true to myself; I stayed cheerful, worked as hard as I could, and kept track of every task I completed so that I could prove to anyone else, and to myself, that I was indeed working as hard as I said I was. I believe that's why I took things so personally, because I take pride in my work, I'm not lazy, and I *loved* my job!

The next time I met with my supervisor, things were different. She was more upbeat, and things were explained to me. I came to understand that my new coworker was struggling, but rather than talking to me or asking for help, he went to our supervisor. And possibly because they are friends, going out drinking together, he felt more comfortable reporting to her that I was not carrying my weight and not supporting him. We were a team, and had I been overwhelmed, I would have asked for help, but that may not have been his way.

My supervisor swayed between friendliness, including me in the conversations, to cold brevity, but I was never invited into discussions for future plans for the office I had worked so hard for this last year. Not being from Hawaii, I was accustomed to not being included in the conversations when so much of it was regarding events the group had gone to together in the past or gossip about mutual friends, but being excluded from workplace plans was incredibly uncomfortable. I felt ill. I did my best to stay cheerful, agreeable, and treat my coworkers with respect. Knowing one way or another that my time was limited, I was sure to express my gratitude and admiration in all sincerity for my coworkers whom I respected.

I saw it coming a mile away; when I was brought into the office, the first meeting I was actually included in on in a month, it came as no surprise that the woman I had cheerfully brought back to meet with my supervisor only moments before was actually the human resources representative whose sole purpose was to quietly usher me out of my position, swiftly ending my one plus year employment.

I was fed the lines, "At this time we have decided not to renew your contract," and "This in no way is a poor reflection of your work performance." When I asked if there was a reason, while my supervisor sat mute across the table, the human resources representative would not elaborate but said it could be any number of reasons including differences of personality. She encouraged me to apply for the posted position in a different department, which I did, and interviewed for, only to discover the same supervisor controlled this new department as well. Although I embraced the idea of working with a new department with the same medical center, I had lost a great deal of respect and trust in this particular supervisor.

When I was "escorted" by my supervisor to my desk to pack my things, I reported to her on all that I had prepared and where everything was located, trying to hide the warble in my voice, and then said goodnight as I walked out. I had cried too many tears by that point to let one fall in front of her; she had to know I knew it was coming.

I kept my cool, I stayed true to myself, and I did not get angry or bitter, at least not on the outside. I called Dustin on the way home feeling like I was on cloud nine. After all that awful anticipation, there was finally a resolution. I felt vindicated that the person who made me question myself as a nurse and made me question my normally upbeat personality with her comments, "I think your attitude takes a toll on others," and "I've been noticing a change in your attitude as well and it hasn't been good for anyone," could not say a single word to my face when it came to ending my employment. Those text messages hit me so hard because they came out of nowhere. I truly enjoyed my job, enjoyed working with patients and my coworkers, and knew that there was more behind those words than what appeared on the surface. As if at some point, it was decided she did not want me in that position anymore, and the easiest option would be to smear my reputation and/or make me uncomfortable enough to quit. Whatever the reason was, I have no desire to spend the majority of my time working in that kind of volatile environment.

All said, it was a pleasant parting and an incredible relief. I was given two weeks paid administrative time, interestingly enough on the last day before I was scheduled to take almost two weeks of vacation. When I was offered the position under the same supervisor two months later, I declined with nothing but gratitude.

The more time that passes, the more I convince myself that maybe my attitude was changing, maybe I could have worked harder or tried more to fit in with my coworkers, or maybe I'm not a good nurse. I am frustrated with myself for questioning my skills and love of my career. I am irritated with myself that I have let someone make me doubt myself. I find great comfort in prayer and the idea that each door closes only so that you will see the open door down the line, the door that leads to a better opportunity and a firm path toward a stable and thriving future.

I learned a few very valuable lessons during this experience. I need to be much more aware of how my coworkers are doing. Although my confidence in my own work performance was strong, I was not supporting those around me as I should have. I learned that I cannot get too comfortable; there will always be preferential treatment when social groups are formed in the workplace. But most importantly, I learned once again the power of prayer. Although I am saddened things went the way they did, that I had to spend almost two gut-wrenching months questioning myself and my career, praying helped me through it. My faith guided me to avoid bitterness or retaliation with harsh words and helped me to stay true to myself.

My friends and family know who I truly am, God knows who I truly am, and that's what really matters.

The Grander Plan

And we know that all things work together
for good to those who love God, to those who
are the called according to His purpose.
—Romans 8:28 (NKJV)

God places me, and everyone, where He wants us to be. I have no doubt. As challenging as it was working for the community health center, it made me a stronger nurse. Through the tears, I learned better how to multitask and how to push myself far beyond my comfort zone. Had I not had that incredibly stressful experience, I don't believe I would have been considered for the position working in vascular surgery. Working with the vascular surgeon was an incredibly educational experience on so many levels. I learned more in such a short period of time about the vascular system than I ever thought possible, how to scrub into surgery and how to stitch up a wound, and I was gifted with an up-close preview of what might be in my future if I were not able to better control my brittle diabetes.

Most of the patients we treated in the office had diabetes and were on dialysis as a result of it being poorly controlled. Countless people were being seen for nonhealing wounds as a result of poor circulation, also due to their poorly controlled diabetes. Some of these people were my age or younger. One was blind, while many were missing limbs. I treated wounds where bones were exposed or toes had turned black and fallen off. Although the severity of the wounds was interesting to me from a medical standpoint, and I was happy to assist these people, the images filled my nightmares; but in my dreams, the wounds were inflicted on my own body by my own disease.

Witnessing the suffering of others and helping however I could also helped me to place more priority on my own health. Being parents, we often neglect our own wellbeing in effort to care for our families, earn a living, and keep the ship afloat. But how could I continue to care for those I love if I was missing limbs, unable to work, requiring dialysis three times a week, and blind?

For almost thirty years, I lived with the certainty that my disease was a life sentence, and knowing how much more difficult life could be, I did my best to keep up my health. I harbored no illusions that a pancreas transplant would ever be an option.

After about four months of working in vascular surgery, I prayed to God, for the first time, to heal me of my diabetes. I had *never* done this. Praying for myself for any reason had seemed selfish to me for so long, but I knew God could do anything, so I prayed. Shortly after, the surgeon and I were talking after a busy clinic day, and I mentioned I was type 1 diabetic. He stated, "I think you'd be a great candidate for a pancreas transplant." This planted the seed in my mind, and I started the ball rolling, researching anew and speaking with my provider and endocrinologist. After tests and meetings, I was set up with the University of California San Francisco Health transplant department. I am currently on the waiting list for a pancreas only transplant, a possible *cure* for my diabetes. More on that another day, but I know in my heart that God put me where I needed to be so that I would better learn the value of life and discover the possibility of a cure.

Peace in Death

We are confident, yes, well pleased
rather to be absent from the body and
to be present with the Lord.
—2 Corinthians 5:8 (NKJV)

I would be remiss if I did not share my experiences working with hospice. It was incredibly humbling, inspiring, and encouraging coming to know the patients and the families and being present for their last moments together.

Interestingly enough, the more challenging aspect of my position was helping the families come to terms with the patient's wishes. Often the patients were ready, ready to say goodbye to this world and ready to say hello to God. I met people of all religious backgrounds, but the acceptance and peace exuded by those who knew they were going to meet Jesus left me with a sense of awe. I would sit and listen to their stories as they relived their memories of victories and loss with shared tears and hugs. It was one of the most rewarding careers I have ever had.

People have asked me how I did it. I have pronounced the passing of too many people to recall, and I am not afraid of death. I have searched for heartbeats and inhaled breaths. I have bathed and dressed the bodies. These tasks were secondary to the primary goals, to bring comfort, to allow these people to pass away with dignity, and to assist the family to care for their loved ones. Caring for the body of someone who has passed is far easier than comforting the loved ones left behind. I quickly learned how to separate myself from my work. I would become close with some of my patients and their families, so it was impossible to not become emotionally attached. At times I would come home in tears, feeling as though I had lost a dear friend. But in most instances, I would be able to separate myself in order to cope with all the emotions while completing what needed to be done.

Although it was difficult to witness suffering, God's glory could always be seen in the end.

Chapter 10

Emergency Preparedness

But if anyone does not provide for his own, and
especially for those of his household, he has denied
the faith and is worse than an unbeliever.
—1 Timothy 5:8 (NKJV)

On the morning of January 13, 2018, while working for hospice, I received a call from the family of one of our patients; they believed he was close to passing away. By the time I made the one-hour drive and arrived at his house, the patient had already died. After confirming he had indeed passed, I sat down to make arrangements. After notifying the police, I called the mortuary. Midconversation with the mortuary, my cell phone, along with the phones of the family members gathered around, sounded with a loud alert. Casually, while still listening, I held my cell phone out so that I could read the message, "Emergency Alert BALLISTIC MISSILE THREAT INBOUND TO HAWAII. SEEK IMMEDIATE SHELTER. THIS IS NOT A DRILL." Looking up at the people all around me having just received the same message, I brought the phone back up to my ear and concluded the conversation. Relating the mortuary's time of arrival to the family, I apologized and calmly excused myself.

As soon as I navigated around all the parked cars on the small property, I called my husband. His strong voice coming across the speakers of my car, he let me know he had also received the message, and we agreed the missile would most likely hit Oahu. Our bigger concern would be fallout. We had food and water stored up, so should we need to take shelter, we would be safe. I let him know I was on my way home.

As I drove along the Kohala Coast, I gazed out over the ocean for any evidence of incoming missiles. I said a prayer for God to calm the fears of those who must be terrified at this time. I asked God to protect those who were in danger. I prayed that I would get home safely to be with my family and thanked God. I was not afraid. I did not panic. I knew God had a plan. Other drivers were swerving, randomly pulling over, or stopping in the middle of the road. People were becoming frantic.

For thirty-eight minutes, all of Hawaii thought we were about to be bombed. At thirty-eight minutes, we all received a follow-up message. It was a mistake, a mistake we would never forget. The alert was accidentally issued over television, radio, and cell phones across all of Hawaii due to a miscommunication during a drill at the Hawaii Emergency Management Agency. What struck me about this occurrence was that once again, knowing God allowed for me to feel an incredible peace in the face of an otherwise distressing event.

Preparing with Diabetes

With all the turmoil caused by COVID-19, the fear of not knowing what comes next or how bad this may become, there is significant comfort in feeling prepared for the worst. Living with a disease that requires daily medication brings a new level of trepidation; what if I run out of medication? What if my preferred medication isn't available? What if I'm too ill to get to the pharmacy to pick up my medication?

I trust that God will provide all that we need. I also believe it is foolish to not prepare for the worst-case scenarios. God has gifted us with the good sense to know how to care for ourselves; it would be reckless to not prepare for what disasters this world may present us with.

Living in Hawaii means we are dependent on daily shipments from overseas for our food, supplies, and medicine. If our island becomes quarantined, talking about the worst-case scenario here, or if the shipments are delayed due to illness or quarantine on the other end, we are essentially cut off. Residing on a tropical island does have its perks of course. We are surrounded by a bounty of wild growing avocados, mangos, guavas, bananas, fish, and wild pigs, just to name a few. Many people here live off grid with solar power and catchment for water. We can garden year-round due to lack of severe weather, so access to food is not as threatening as it could be given the seclusion of our islands. The access to medication, however, has the potential to be a major concern.

Stocking up on prescription medication is not a simple thing. Health insurance makes it near impossible to acquire extra supplies, so oftentimes paying cash becomes the only other option, that is, if the medication is available sans prescription. Insulin-dependent diabetics do have that luxury. We can purchase supplies over the counter without a prescription, but the cost of insulin is exorbitant. If you have the cash, great! If not, let me share my strategy with you.

In almost three decades of living with a diagnosis of DM type 1, I have spent far too little of that time in excellent control. My ravenous sweet tooth and emotional eating have made maintaining an optimal hemoglobin A1C a constant challenge. But amidst the ups and downs, weight fluctuations, diet experimentation, and fitness fads, I have learned quite clearly what works for my body and what doesn't. I have discovered when I lose weight, my insulin needs decrease. When I am using less insulin, I am more sensitive to what I use. So in order to decrease my insulin requirement and thereby slowly save my insulin, I cut way down on my carbohydrate intake. Processed carbohydrates such as bread, cereal, and pasta pack the heaviest punch and raise my blood sugar the most, for the longest duration, so that's the first thing to go. Conveniently, cutting back on the carbs also helps me to slowly lose weight, thereby decreasing my need for the long-acting insulin. This is a very gradual process and will not save a massive amount, but it will help.

Along with the processed carbohydrates, I also cut back on starchy vegetables and fruit. I do not eliminate these foods completely because there is a great deal of benefit in them, and their impact on my blood sugar is much less significant if taken in moderation. The sugar has got to go though, no getting around that. The candy, sugared dried fruit, and alcohol are out.

Exercise plays a huge role in my plan as well. My long days at work and the importance of enough sleep have limited my opportunities for long workouts, so I catch what time I can for a walk, some lunges, pushups, the spin bike, and a run when I can. This is not only important for the more obvious reasons—cardiovascular health, etc.—but also because it speeds up my metabolism and thereby decreases my need for insulin.

While my insulin needs decrease, my body becomes leaner and stronger, and my overall health improves, my insulin prescription *does not* change. I am able to save, or stock up if you will, on my insulin. Yes, insulin expires, but not nearly as quickly as the pharmaceutical companies would have you believe. And I speak from experience here, not medical expertise. Over time, insulin loses its effectiveness but does not spontaneously expire, become poisonous, or any such nonsense. So in the event I find myself using insulin two months or two years past its expiration date, I would test my blood sugar more frequently and make adjustments initially till I'm sure it is having its desired effect.

My husband Dustin is a god-sent in so many ways. Preparing ourselves for worst-case scenarios is one of his many gifts. It would be foolish for us to assume "all will turn out for the best" without doing the work first. God created us with the ability to think for ourselves, to research all possibilities, and to prepare for outcomes that may not be the most comfortable. Trusting our fellow man is a beautiful act, but in today's time of derision, ungodliness, and outright disregard for the value of human life, I believe God needs us to be prepared to be self-sufficient and to be able to protect and provide for ourselves, all while following His Word.

Chapter 11

Taking a Pause

*In this you greatly rejoice, though now for a
little while, if need be, you have been grieved
by various trials, that the genuineness of your
faith, being much more precious than gold that
perishes, though it is tested by fire, may be found
to praise, honor, and glory at the revelation of
Jesus Christ, whom having not seen you love.*
—1 Peter 1:6 (NKJV)

I feel blessed beyond all measure to know that I have heard *the calling.* I have felt called to share my experiences with my various health issues. I have felt called to discuss my history of emotional roller coasters. I have felt called to review our adventures in fostering, however brief they have been thus far. But most importantly, I have been called to share the love I have for God and the love God has for us all with all of you.

So what adventures do we have planned for the future? Emily Rogers has inspired me to no end. She piloted a nonprofit called Hanai Ministries (hanaiministries.org), which I have joined on to help out with in any way I can. She has amazing ideas for how to help the less fortunate families and foster children on our island, with special goals for the foster children with health problems and special needs. These children are particularly difficult to place with stable, qualified families and often spend their time in group homes hardly situated to provide them with the care and love they deserve and so desperately need. This cause speaks to me as a nurse and as a mother. Myself and other kind souls from our church, Hamakua Baptist, have joined the governing board of Hanai Ministries to help these children by educating others on the dire fostering situation on Hawaii Island and providing resources however possible. We hope to be a resource to help struggling families attain the things they need to help fosters, as well as to provide for their own family if in difficult situations.

Our current situation has left me without a job. Rather than feeling hopeless or purposeless, I have been rejuvenated with the spark of an old purpose's flame burning anew within me. This time off work has been an amazing gift, although unexpected, and I am making the most of it. I still feel young. I know there are many years ahead of me and many adventures to be had. Like a letter I begin with grand intentions, only to never finish and never send, I know if I don't pause my tale here, I may never share it with the world. It's not an extravagant tale, but it's mine. My heart overflows with gratitude that I can know Jesus as I do, and I look forward to all the amazing ways my relationship will grow in the coming years. Then perhaps our family will have a new story to share.

But for me and my home, we will serve the Lord. (Joshua 24:15 NKJV)

About the Author

Rachel grew up in San Diego, California, and moved to Hawaii with her husband and two children in 2014, looking to escape the busy city and focus more on family. She has since learned to love a more simple life and rediscovered her passion for writing while developing a closer relationship with God.

Rachel has been a nurse for over a decade and has enjoyed her experience in hospice and vascular surgery. She served on the school board of her children's school, starting a parent–teacher group, and now homeschools her son and teenage daughter. As a family, Rachel and her children care for their chickens and vegetable garden, learning the value of self-reliance.

She and her husband became foster parents in 2019 to help the children of Hawaii upon learning of the dire fostering situation on the island. She enjoys volunteering with her church and serves on the board of Hanai Ministries while teaching her children the importance of serving God and helping others. In her spare time, she loves surfing with her daughter, staying active, writing, participating in fundraising events, and adventuring with her family.

You can read more about Rachel and her aspirations at hanai-ministeries.org and on her blog at joyfulchaos.blog.

CPSIA information can be obtained
at www.ICGtesting.com
Printed in the USA
BVHW071055160822
644711BV00007B/403